Advanced interactive interfaces with Access

Building Interactive Interfaces with VBA

Alessandro Grimaldi

Apress®

Advanced interactive interfaces with Access: Building Interactive Interfaces with VBA

Alessandro Grimaldi
Frankfurt am Main, Germany

ISBN-13 (pbk): 979-8-8688-0807-4   ISBN-13 (electronic): 979-8-8688-0808-1
https://doi.org/10.1007/979-8-8688-0808-1

Managing Director, Apress Media LLC: Welmoed Spahr
Acquisitions Editor: Smriti Srivastava
Development Editor: Laura Berendson
Editorial Assistant: Kripa Joseph

Cover designed by eStudioCalamar

Cover image designed by Freepik (www.freepik.com)

Distributed to the book trade worldwide by Springer Science+Business Media New York, 1 New York Plaza, Suite 4600, New York, NY 10004-1562, USA. Phone 1-800-SPRINGER, fax (201) 348-4505, e-mail orders-ny@springer-sbm.com, or visit www.springeronline.com. Apress Media, LLC is a California LLC and the sole member (owner) is Springer Science + Business Media Finance Inc (SSBM Finance Inc). SSBM Finance Inc is a **Delaware** corporation.

For information on translations, please e-mail booktranslations@springernature.com; for reprint, paperback, or audio rights, please e-mail bookpermissions@springernature.com.

Apress titles may be purchased in bulk for academic, corporate, or promotional use. eBook versions and licenses are also available for most titles. For more information, reference our Print and eBook Bulk Sales web page at http://www.apress.com/bulk-sales.

Any source code or other supplementary material referenced by the author in this book is available to readers on GitHub. For more detailed information, please visit https://www.apress.com/gp/services/source-code.

If disposing of this product, please recycle the paper

To my parents. Nothing would have been possible without them.

Table of Contents

About the Author ix

About the Technical Reviewers xi

Acknowledgments xiii

Introduction xv

Chapter 1: Writing Code: Good Practices and Tips 1

1.1. Option Explicit 2

1.2. Option Compare 3

1.3. Variable Names 4

1.4. Private/Public 7

1.5. User-Defined Types (UDT)..9

1.6. Service Functions 11

1.7. Boolean Parameters..12

1.8. Optional Parameters 16

1.9. Control Names 17

1.10. Control Tags 18

1.11. Function Exit Point 19

1.12. Function Returning Value 21

1.13. Indenting, Spacing, Commenting 23

1.14. Object Destruction 28

1.15. Wall of Declarations 29

1.16. Dim ... As New 32

1.17. Make `Variant` Explicit 34

1.18. `Boolean` and `Date` Data Type 34

1.19. SELECT CASE 36

1.20. `Call` Instruction 39

1.21. Feedback 41

1.22. Conclusion 41

Chapter 2: VBA Classes 43

2.1. Creating a Class 46

2.2. Instantiating a Class.. 47

2.3. Properties... 49

2.4. Methods 54

2.5. "Companion" Module 55

2.6. Nested Classes 57

2.7. Conclusion 63

Chapter 3: The Presence Vector Technique 65

3.1. Conclusion 86

Chapter 4: Advanced Interfaces: Drag and Drop 87

4.1. How to Make an Image Draggable... 88

4.2. Adding More Images 104

4.3. Connecting Two Images with Lines... 108

4.4. Connecting Multiple Images 127

4.5. The "Ghost Label" Technique 150

4.6. Sliding Forms 164

4.7. Conclusion 185

Chapter 5: Advanced Interfaces: Scrollable Timeline.....................187

    5.1. Design the Timeline 188

    5.2. Make It Scrollable 191

    5.3. Add Navigation Controls..216

    5.4. Placing Objects 227

    5.5. Conclusion 267

Chapter 6: Outro 269

Index...271

About the Author

Alessandro Grimaldi was born in Rome, Italy, where he first approached the computer world in 1982. He has been a professional VBA developer since 1998. For several years, Alessandro consulted for the World Food Programme (WFP), a major United Nations agency for which he worked in Afghanistan, North Korea, Ethiopia, and Italy. He has also worked in Vienna, Austria, for the CTBTO, another UN agency. Since 2014, he has lived in Frankfurt, Germany, where he worked for the European Central Bank for about five years. In all these places, he has developed VBA tools, ranging from simple automation tools to complex, multiuser, distributed, enterprise-level applications.

In recent years, Alessandro has produced several videos about drag and drop and the scrolling timeline and delivered live workshops and presentations explaining these techniques. He has an online VBA shop (AlessandroGrimaldi.com/Shop) where he sells VBA tutorials, workshops, and tools. He also has a YouTube channel (@AlxGrim) where he publishes VBA-related videos.

About the Technical Reviewers

Simone Bardi, a database solution designer and developer, has over 20 years of national and international experience in developing tools for data collection, monitoring, and analysis for organizations such as the United Nations World Food Programme (Afghanistan and Italy), UN International Organization for Migration, European Central Bank (Germany), and Vodafone Italy, among others.

Simone has a strong background in MS Access databases (VBA) and MS Excel applications (VBA) for data collection and analysis as well as in cyber security, with many years of experience in ICT security in the private telecommunications sector, focusing on GDPR-related matters, data protection, and fraud prevention.

Colin Riddington has been an Access developer for over 25 years, with many years creating database solutions for schools in the United Kingdom. After taking early retirement from teaching, he set up his own company, Mendip Data Systems, to focus on database development and consultancy. He has been awarded Microsoft Most Valuable Professional (MVP) status for the past three years, starting in 2022. Colin is co-president of the Access Europe user group and a member of the Access Forever team. He is also active on many forums with the username Isladogs. Colin's Isladogs on Access website includes many Access articles, example apps, sample code, and security challenges, together with commercial applications for businesses, schools, and developers. He also runs his own YouTube channel. His focus is on stretching the boundaries of what can be achieved using Access.

Acknowledgments

There are several people I have to thank, who somehow contributed not only to this book but to my work in general.

Stefano Valenzi[1] has been a brother to me for the last 30 years, always helping me and supporting me with his immense knowledge and experience. He gave me the idea to write this book.

Simone Bardi[2] is a good friend of mine. His VBA and logical skills helped me a lot in developing my initial interfaces, and I still call him whenever I need a second brain. He's one of the reviewers of this book.

Karl Donaubauer (Access MVP),[3] the "great guru" of the Access community worldwide. In 2021, he invited me to talk about my work at his Access Developer Conference that year, and since then, my career has taken a decisive turn.

Colin Riddington (Access MVP),[4] the second reviewer of this book. I consider him my mentor and my guide in the complex world of online meetings. Extremely supportive toward me, he did me the honor of nominating me cochairman of AUG Europe.

David Nealey[5] is a fan of my work, and I do admire his. With almost no line of code, he can create amazing infocharts in his Access applications. He's always been very supportive toward me, even choosing me as his cochairman for his LinkedIn group "Modern Access Design."

---

[1] www.linkedin.com/in/StefanoValenzi/
[2] www.linkedin.com/in/SimoneBardi/
[3] www.donkarl.com/
[4] https://isladogs.co.uk/
[5] www.linkedin.com/in/DNealey/

Introduction

In April 2021, I was invited to the Access Developer Conference (DevCon), probably the biggest and most important gathering of Access developers from all around the world (well, mainly the United States and Europe). Karl Donaubauer (25 times MVP, at the moment I'm writing), the organizer, had happened to see some of my Access works on the Web and asked me to show them at the convention. Despite my previous decades of activity, that was my first exposure to the international Access community, and I didn't really know what to expect. But it went very well; my work received a lot of compliments, and no one in the audience mentioned they had already seen anything similar. Apparently, I had created something new! During the convention, I met David Nealey, a talented Access developer who creates amazing charts in Access practically without code, something that has always amazed me. He forged the term "Access on steroids" to highlight the originality and the visual impact of my interfaces.

I am somehow the opposite of David: I write tons of code, and sometimes I write code to do operations that Access does by default just because I like to have control on every single bit (pun intended) of my applications. And I like to experiment. In the early 2000s, I had this weird idea of experimenting on interactive interfaces with Access, and eventually, the first "drag-and-drop" engine was born. Since then, I have applied this basic engine to almost all of the applications I've been developing through the years, with several variations and improvements, always experimenting, always trying to go "beyond," always pushing Access to its limits.

Why this book? During the last few years, I produced several tutorials and workshops (check my YouTube channel and my online VBA shop), but I eventually decided to collect everything in one single place to reduce the fragmentation and explain things in a more coherent way. I tried to make things as clear as possible, to reach not only the experienced developers but also those with a more limited experience who want to dive deeper into this amazing programming language – even though, of course, a full and solid knowledge of VBA is absolutely required, as the goal of this book is NOT teaching VBA.

We'll start with a quick overview of my favorite "best practices" and a short digression on VBA classes. And that's because in the third part, when I discuss some of my favorite dynamic interfaces, I will make large use of those very personal conventions, which (I'm aware) don't match the more common, "mainstream" conventions. So you'll know what to expect.

I said *dynamic* interfaces: that's how I like to call what I do, more than *graphical* interfaces, because at the end of the day, every interface is graphical, but mine does something more, since there's a lot of things moving, and they allow the user to interact with the objects on the screen, pretty much like Windows does.

One final note: I'm Italian. I studied English mostly by myself, and I'm sadly aware that my English is quite far from being perfect. This means that in this book, you'll find mistakes, wrong words, and expressions that may sound strange to an English native speaker. I refuse to use ChatGPT or any other AI tools to correct it because I still like to use my own brain and I'm not yet ready to turn it off. I just beg you to be so kind as to bear with it – but if you find something really horrible and incomprehensible, please let me know, and I'll be happy to correct it!

Well, I hope you may find at least some interesting input in these pages, and I kindly ask you to mention my name, should you implement in your applications any of the techniques explained here.

CHAPTER 1

Writing Code: Good Practices and Tips

…where I explain my coding conventions, which will be used throughout the entire book.

There is an old saying that goes: "Write your code as if your replacement is a psycho killer." The meaning should be clear: your code should be comprehensible, well written, and easy to understand and modify. Whoever is given the task to read and edit it, you won't want him to get angry with you because you left him with an incomprehensible bunch of messy lines.

Of course, this is slippery ground. We all have a different mind and, above all, a different concept of "order." What is perfectly clear to me may be totally absurd for another programmer. That is why what follows is by no means a list of "best" practices and tips: it's just a list of "good" practices and tips that have been working well for me in the last decades. Depending on your experience, some *are* obvious, some *may* be obvious, and some may be *less* obvious. In any case, I'm not claiming you *must* embed them in your programming style: all I'm saying is that they proved to be reasonable habits, and I hope that some of them may make some sense to some of you. In any case, I'm going to use *these* conventions in the rest of the book, as I'm going to show you *my* original code.

A. Grimaldi, *Advanced interactive interfaces with Access*,
https://doi.org/10.1007/979-8-8688-0808-1_1

1.1. Option Explicit

I always use the `Option Explicit` clause at the top of every module. *Always*. This forces me to declare (`Dim`) every single variable I use in my code, allowing VBA to check if the values I assign them are compatible with their declared type. This can dramatically reduce some kinds of errors – for example, syntax errors. Consider the following fragment of code:

```
Public Sub Multiply(num1, num2)
    Debug.print numl * num2
End Sub
```

Of course, this is very basic, but it's just to illustrate the point. If you call the function (e.g., from the Immediate Window), you will always get a result of 0. Can you understand why? If you look closer, you will notice that the first parameter of the function is <num1> (N-U-M-**1**), while inside the function, it's misspelled as <numl> (N-U-M-**L**). Finding these kinds of errors may be rather difficult and time-consuming, particularly if the misspelled variable is a global one and appears several times throughout your code.

What happens if we use `Option Explicit`? When we run the function (or when we compile the code), the execution stops, the misspelled variable is highlighted, and an error message box says "Variable not defined."

There are even subtler errors that may occur due, for example, to a variable name used twice in different contexts, maybe holding different value types, etc. The list of errors that can be avoided using `Option Explicit` is too long to mention: I just use it every time and strongly suggest you do the same.

1.2. Option Compare

Strangely enough, many VBA programmers disregard this statement, which automatically appears as the very first line of each new code module. Yet, it's an important statement that can dramatically change the behavior of our code, so it's a good thing to thoroughly understand how it works. It basically has to do with string comparisons, for example, in `If` statements. Its parameter has three possible values:

`Option Compare Database`

This option is only available in Access (not in Excel, Word, etc.). Practically speaking, the string comparison is based on the sort order determined by the local international settings, so it follows the rules of the local language.

`Option Compare Text`

The comparison is performed on a case-insensitive basis, so "John" and "john" are considered the same string.

`Option Compare Binary (default)`

The comparison is based on the binary representation of the characters – practically, their ASCII codes. In this context, "John" and "john" are different.

An additional note of the term "default," which in this case can be a little confusing. When you create a module, Access adds `Option Compare Database` on the first line, so this is actually a kind of "default." The point is that if you remove that line, and if you don't make explicit which of the three methods you're using, Access assumes it's the `Binary,` which makes it the real "default."

Choosing one or the other of these statements can make a substantial difference. The results of your code can be greatly impacted, so you should pay some attention to this choice. For example, if your code checks for duplicates, you'll probably have something like `if (newName = oldName) then....` This kind of instruction is influenced by the `Option Compare` directive, and you may or may not want to consider the different letter cases.

A real-life example (it happened to me!): I was checking the field names of a recordset, and something kept going wrong. I finally realized that the test `fld.Name = "Title"` kept failing because the actual field name was `title` and there was no `Option Compare` directive specified – so `Option Compare Binary` was active. Lesson learned.

1.3. Variable Names

Sometimes we tend to be lazy and name variables with short, meaningless names: `tID`, `clNo`, `pAvg`, and such. This is NOT a good practice. Even though they can be extremely clear in your mind, it makes the code hard to read, hard to understand, and almost impossible for anyone to follow your procedures. And this includes YOU if you happen to look back again to your code after a few months.

Spend some more time, but give your variables comprehensible names: `tempID`, `clientNumber`, `priceAverage`, and so on. It may be OK to use a name like `i` when you run a loop:

```
For i = 1 to 10
```

It's a rather standard practice, and no one will blame you for that. Of course, a more meaningful name is always well accepted, for example:

```
For clientNdx = 1 to 10
```

is definitely better.

Talking about variable naming, there are two vexed questions:

1. *What case should I use?*

    Basically, there are four styles which are widely used:

    Snake Case: number_of_registered_clients

    Letters are all lowercase, and words are separated by an underscore character. It's typically used in Python. A variation is the so-called "Screaming Snake Case," with all capital letters such as in NUMBER_OF_REGISTERED_CLIENTS.

    Personally, I do not like it very much, as you need to type the extra character "_" for each word. Typically, I use the "Screaming Snake Case" to declare constants only.

    Kebab case: number-of-registered-clients

    Like the previous one, it just uses a dash instead of an underscore. You see a lot of that in web addresses. It goes without saying that I do not like it either because of the extra characters. Anyway, it's not accepted in VBA.

    Pascal case: NumberOfRegisteredClients

    No additional characters, here: every word is capitalized, so it's easy to see where a word ends and another begins. This style is widely used, especially for naming classes. And this could be my favorite, if it wasn't for the fourth style...

    Camel Case: numberOfRegisteredClients

What's the difference? The first letter, which is in lowercase. This style is especially used in Java and Javascript for creating functions, methods, and variable names. Why do I prefer this? I don't know, really. It's just a personal preference, without a rational explanation.

Whichever style you decide is best for you, the important thing is that you maintain coherence throughout your whole application. Mixing styles may be confusing and definitely gives a sense of disorder, inaccuracy, and superficiality.

2. *Do I have to add a prefix to explicit the variable type?*

   This discussion has always been very popular. If I declare the variable `itemNumber` as an integer, do I have to name it `intItemNumber`? If I declare `clientName` as a string, should I actually name it `strClientName`? Well, in my opinion, the answer is a resounding *no*. If you choose the name wisely, most of the times the prefix is useless. I mean, `clientName` is obviously a string. `isOK` is clearly a Boolean, so do we really need to name it `blnIsOk`? `itemCodeNumber` is a number, intuitively an integer or a long (does it really matter? Do you make calculations on item code numbers?). I think these prefixes reduce the readability, overloading the code with (mostly) useless information.

   Some cases are borderline, I know. For example, `itemCode` is an integer, a long, a string, or what? Well, it's not that important to me. Once I see that `itemCode` is declared as a string, I do not find it too difficult to remember it when I meet this variable in the code. But again, this is how MY mind works. Yours may very well be very different and appreciate those extra characters in every occurrence of your variables.

1.4. Private/Public

We all know that a variable or a function defined in a code module is always public. And we all know that in a form module, a variable or a function is private by default. But I think it's a very good practice to always make it explicit. So, in a module, I never write

```
Sub somePublicSub()
    [...]
End Sub
```

but I always go for

```
Public Sub somePublicSub()
    [...]
End Sub
```

Similarly, for the private routines, I always write

```
Private Sub somePrivateSub()
    [...]
End Sub
```

I think it makes everything much clearer and unambiguous.

And if I have a lot of subs/functions, sometimes I go one step further and prefix `loc` (for *local*) to all private routines:

```
Private Sub locSomePrivateSub()
    [...]
End Sub
```

This way, in the procedure combo box, they will be all grouped together, and it's easier to tell a public function from a private one, as shown in Figure 1-1.

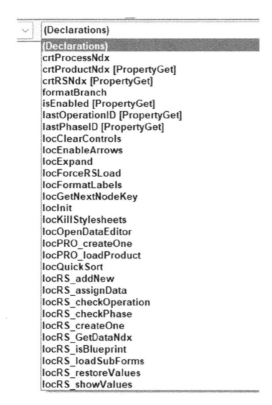

Figure 1-1. *List of procedures*

1.5. User-Defined Types (UDT)

Most of the problems with variable names disappear when you use UDTs.
A UDT looks like this:

```
Private Type recClient
    clientName As String
    Code As String
    officeNumber As String
    personalMobileNumber As String
    officeMobileNumber As String
    Date as Long
End Type
Private Client as recClient
```

Why are UDTs so great? For several reasons:

- They allow you to group a coherent set of variables
  (as many as you need) under one single name (in the
  previous example, Client). You only need to remember
  that name and forget about the many single variables.

- You exploit VBA's Intellisense engine. When you type
  Client. (with a dot) in your code, you can see all the
  variables inside the structure. You can select one with
  the keyboard arrows or just type its first letters and then
  hit TAB.

- For this reason, you can use longer and more
  meaningful names (see the two telephone numbers
  in the preceding example) since you do not have to
  remember them nor to type them.

- A medium project can have dozens of variables. It's easy to forget one or two of them, and you may forget to update them when needed. This can't happen with a UDT since you always have the list of all the variables at a glance.

- In a UDT, you can also use names that normally are forbidden, as they are part of the standard VBA syntax, such as Date in the preceding example. And this is possible because since they are enclosed in a higher level structure, there's no space for ambiguity: Access knows that a reference to Date and a reference to Client.Date are two different things.

Personally, I always use a (public) UDT named recGlobals in all my projects, in a module, collecting all the global variables. Then I declare

```
Public Globals as recGlobals.
```

And that immensely helps me keep track of my global variables (which in a big application can be *a lot*), to reduce typos, and to make the code more readable. Besides, in every form module, I always use a similar technique for the local variables, defining

```
Private Type recLocals
    [...]
End Type
Private Locals As recLocals
```

Side note: Why do I prefix rec to a UDT name? Historical reasons. In 1987, I had to work with COBOL, and COBOL had this type of structured data, called "record," extremely similar to a UDT in VBA. I used the "rec" prefix a lot, to name those records, and I kept this habit when I moved to VBA.

1.6. Service Functions

A *service* (or *convenience*) *function* is a small function that performs a single, specific task; it doesn't really matter if big (tens of lines) or small (one single line). For example:

- Performs a calculation with numbers or dates

- Builds a string according to a complex pattern

- Reads a value from a table

- Initializes a set of variables

- Enables/disables controls on a form

A service function can be very useful, in case you need it several times. For example, the following function is only one line long, but it's extremely useful to generate a pseudo-random ID with max four digits:

```
Public Function getRandomID() As Long
    getRandomID = Int(Rnd(Timer - Int(Timer)) * 10000)
End Function
```

If you need to generate IDs in your application, remembering and retyping this line several times can be frustrating, boring, and prone to errors. Instead, you can call getRandomID() and forget about the details. Moreover, if one day you decide to change the formula that generates the ID, you will only have to change it once, in this function, leaving the rest of the code unaltered, and all generated IDs will keep their consistency.

If you make such functions Public, they become in all respects like a native VBA function, which you can use anywhere in your code, or query, or report, or even in a form control. So, don't be shy, use them often, and appreciate their advantages:

- You do not have to write the same stuff over and over.

- Type less, thus reducing typos and errors.

11

- You do not have to remember long/complex formulas or code snippets.

- Easier code maintenance and modification.

- Easier coherence and consistency control.

- Code readability (a function name vs. complex code).

1.7. Boolean Parameters

Sometimes, a function needs many parameters, where "many" may vary from person to person, but for me, it means three or four. In my mind, if a function needs more parameters than that, something might be wrong, and the code might need to be restructured. Of course, this is not always the case: a function MAY actually need a higher number of parameters.

In many cases, though, it's not real parameters you need to pass but rather True/False values. For example, if you have a function that formats a date into a string, you may want to be very flexible and specify the following options:

- Show/hide the leading zeros (e.g., 01-09-2024 vs. 1-9-2024)

- Show/hide the year (e.g., 01-09-2024 vs. 01-09)

- Show/hide the day (e.g., 01-09-2024 vs. 09-2024)

- Use two digits for the year instead of four (e.g., 24 vs. 2024)

- Show/hide the time (e.g., 01-09-2024 09:46:23 vs. 01-09-2024)

- Show/hide the seconds (e.g., 09:46:23 vs. 09:46)

- Use AM/PM rather than a 24-hour clock (e.g., 07:00:00 PM vs. 19:00:00)

And of course, you may think of even more formatting options. Now, normally you would specify a parameter for each of these options. This, of course, would be a terrible choice. The function signature would look like

```
Function formatDate(dt As Date, _
            leadingZeros As Boolean, _
            showYear As Boolean, _
            showDay As Boolean, _
            use4DigitYear As Boolean, _
            hideTime As Boolean, _
            showSeconds As Boolean, _
            useAM_PM_Format As Boolean) As String
End Function
```

plus, other necessary parameters such as the date format (e.g., DD/MM/ YY), the separator (colon, space, dash, etc.), and maybe more, which would obviously result in a huge, unacceptable signature.

I saw many applications where the developer solved the problem by creating a class, using these pieces of info as properties. Frankly, to me, this looks like shooting a fly with a cannon. A UDT would be sufficient.

Or, we can use a binary-based technique usually called "bit-field." Since we'll examine this technique later in this book, this can be a good occasion to see a possible application of it. In a nutshell, the bit-field technique considers the binary representation of a number: since each bit can be either 0 or 1, it can be seen as a "presence indicator" for a set of items. Each bit is logically associated with one specific item. If the bit is 0, the value of its associated item is False; if the bit is 1, the associated value is True. Let's see how this can help in this case. Consider this enumeration:

```
Enum enmDateOptions
    doLEADING_ZEROS = 1
    doSHOW_YEAR = 2
    doSHOW_DAY = 4
```

```
    doTWO_DIGIT_YEAR = 8
    doSHOW_TIME = 16
    doSHOW_SECONDS = 32
    doUSE_AM_PM = 64
End Enum
```

It's my habit to name an enumeration with the enm prefix and a two-word name (in this case, DateOptions). Each value is then prefixed with the initials of these two words (in this case, do). This makes it easier, when I write the code, to remember which enumeration each value belongs to.

Note how each item has a value which is a power of 2. We won't dive into the details of the binary system for now: all you need to understand here is that this set of values guarantees that every combination (sum) of values is unique. For example, the number 98 can only be obtained by

```
doUSE_AM_PM + doSHOW_SECONDS + doSHOW_YEAR
```

and no other combination can give the same value. The new signature for the function will then be

```
Function formatDate(dt As Date, Options As enmDateOptions)
As String
```

which is much more readable than the previous one with eight parameters. How do we call this function? Here's an example:

```
result = formatDate (Date(), doLEADING_ZEROS Or doSHOW_YEAR
Or doSHOW_DAY)
```

The body of the function will check the value of Options and take actions accordingly. In our example:

```
Function formatDate(dt As Date, Options As enmDateOptions)
As String
    if (Options And doLEADING_ZEROS) then ...
    if (Options And doSHOW_YEAR) then ...
```

```
if (Options And doSHOW_DAY) then ...
if ...
End Function
```

According to the binary math, the AND operation returns 0 if Options does not contain the tested value, otherwise returns a nonzero value (more precisely, the value itself). So, in our example:

```
Options And doLEADING_ZEROS = doLEADING_ZEROS (≠0)
Options And doSHOW_YEAR = doSHOW_YEAR (≠0)
Options And doSHOW_DAY = doSHOW_DAY (≠0)
```

but:

```
Options And doTWO_DIGIT_YEAR = 0
Options And do_SHOW_TIME = 0
```

and so on, so the associated if actions won't be executed.

And the best thing is that every time an enumeration value is required, the Intellisense engine shows a list of all the available values, so you do not have to remember them, as shown in Figure 1-2.

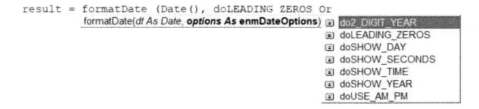

Figure 1-2. *UDT components*

Now, why Or and not +? In this case, the two symbols are equivalent. But I always prefer to use Or in place of the plus sign when I'm dealing with Boolean values because it's more logical and because, in some cases, they produce different results. We'll talk in more detail about this topic in the chapter dedicated to this technique.

Its advantages should nonetheless be already clear:

- Compact signatures.

- Code readability in function calls (meaningful constant names rather than a long series of TRUE/FALSE).

- Scalability and flexibility: You can add enumeration values, but the signature and all the calls to the function remain the same because the number of parameters (two in this case) doesn't change.

1.8. Optional Parameters

Do you ever use the OPTIONAL clause in a function signature? Sometimes it's very handy, especially when you find out you need an extra parameter in the middle of your development and do not want to break the existing code. You add the parameter as OPTIONAL, and all the code will keep working. Or, more commonly, you do not want to specify the same parameter over and over every time you call that function, so you declare it as OPTIONAL giving it that value as default.

```
Function someName(parm1 As Integer, Optional parm2 As
Integer = 0)
```

Personally, I tend to avoid this clause, though. The problem is that when you compile the code, you won't catch all those calls that do NOT specify the optional parameter. So, it's very much possible that sooner or later, you call the function without specifying the optional parameter even when you should and never be aware of that. The output may be wrong, but you may never notice that, and keep thinking that everything is fine – until someone realizes that there's a problem, and this is never a good thing. I'm very careful when it comes to using OPTIONAL, and usually, I prefer to take some more time to call the function with all its parameters, every time.

1.9. Control Names

Each control on a form should get a proper name. The default names (such as TextBox1 or Label23) do not say much and make the code extremely difficult to understand, update, and maintain. As per what name convention is "the best," this is another difficult answer to give, much like it was when we talked about variable names. The common approach is to prefix three letters to the given name, to clarify what kind of control we're talking about and append a meaningful name. So, for example, we can call a textbox txtClientName and a label lblAddress.

Here is a list of the prefixes I personally use, for the most used controls:

Text box	txt
Label	lbl
Command button	cmd
Tab control	tab
Combo box	cmb
Toggle	tog
Listbox	lst
Check box	chk
Image	img
Form	msk
Subform	smsk

You can notice I make an exception to the three-letter rule for subforms. Programmers usually do not like exceptions, but I can live with that. But most of all, I use msk (for "mask" [1]) instead of the most common frm, and that's because I use frm for frames. Just a matter of habit.

Whatever your choice, as usual, be consistent.

1.10. Control Tags

Like names, control tags are very important. Incredibly, not everyone knows that every single control has a tag property and even less know how to use it. And yet, tags are one of the more powerful tools that Access has to offer at design time. You can use tags in a number of ways to group controls or to store valuable information. For example, suppose you have a set of controls you want to enable or disable according to some user input. Let's say that when the user clears a certain check box, a whole section of the form must be disabled and enabled again if the check box is ticked. Of course, if we're talking about a few controls, we can address them individually:

```
Control1.Enabled = False
Control2.Enabled = False
...
ControlN.Enabled = False
```

But what if there are ten, twelve, or more controls? The code would be uselessly long and hard to maintain. A good solution would be to set all those control tags to the same value, say, VISIBILITY. The code would then be reduced to three lines only:

```
For Each ctl In Me.Controls
    If (ctl.Tag = "VISIBILITY") Then ctl.Visible = False
Next
```

_____

[1] It's worth noting that in Italian a form is usually called _maschera_, that is, _mask_. That's where _msk_ comes from.

18

And that's a scalable solution: it will work with no modifications even if you remove or add (with the proper tag) controls on the form.

Another possible use of tags is to store information. For example, in a command button tag, you can store a compound string with these pieces of information:

```
[name of the form to open]@[form caption]
```

To make a practical example, the tag may look like

```
mskSettings@Application Settings
```

And the click event may look like

```
Private Sub cmdSettings_Click()
    DoCmd.OpenForm Split(cmdSettings, "@")(0), _
                        OpenArgs:=Split(cmdSettings, "@")(1)
End Sub
```

This is just a silly example, but this method can be used in more complex situations. And do not forget that the tag property can be dynamically changed via code at run time, providing a lot of flexibility.

1.11. Function Exit Point

The exit point of a function is the line of code where a function ends, returning whatever value it's supposed to return. Apparently, it's a common habit to write functions with many exit points, something like

```
Function foo()
    foo = [some value]
    [...]
    if (...) then exit function        ' 1
    [...]
```

```
    if (...) then
        foo = [some other value]
        Exit Function                    ' 2
    End If

    foo = [yet another value]         ' 3
End Function
```

This function has three exit points (lines 1, 2, 3). This is an extremely bad programming style. A function should have one and only one exit point – a very good practice that dramatically reduces runtime errors and makes debugging easier. GoTo can help a lot here. I know there is a lot of reluctance to use this instruction because at school we were taught that it "breaks the execution flow" and makes the code "unstructured." Well, that is absolutely true if it's used carelessly. But in a few, well-controlled cases, it's a very friendly instruction that makes more good than bad. Our previous example could be rewritten like this:

```
Function foo()
    foo = [some value]
    [...]
    if (...) then GoTo exitMe
    [...]

    if (...) then
        foo = [some other value]
        GoTo exitMe
    End If

    foo = [yet another value]

exitMe:
    [Code to run when the function ends]      ' 1

End Function
```

The GoTo thing doesn't cause much harm here, but it provides one single exit point to the function (line 1), simplifying debugging and editing. Not only that, but it happens quite often that when a function ends, there are several operations to be performed: objects must be destroyed, variables must be set, pop-up messages must be shown, maybe other functions must be called, and so on. Providing a single exit point makes sure that all this code is written and invoked only once – again, for the sake of readability, simplicity, and maintenance.

1.12. Function Returning Value

A function returns a value, and the function name is used for this purpose. Additionally, the function name can be used within the function itself as if it was a variable, as we saw a moment ago. Another example:

```
Function doubleIt(n as Long) As Long
    doubleIt = 2 * n
    If (doubleIt > MAX) then
        MsgBox "..."
        doubleIt = doubleIt / 2
    End If
End Function
```

Now, this is a bit weird, I know, but that's how my brain works: *I don't like this feature.* I find it rather confusing and hard to follow, debug, and maintain. What I do 99% of the time is using a local variable called retVal, which is used in the calculations in the function body and is assigned to the function name only at the very end:

```
Function doubleIt(n as Long) As Long
dim retVal as Long

    retVal = 2 * n
```

```
If (retVal > MAX) then
    MsgBox "..."
    retVal = retVal / 2
End If

doubleIt = retVal
```

```
End Function
```

I find it's even better when coupled with what we said a moment ago, about the single exit point. The previous example becomes

```
Function foo()
    retVal = [some value]
    [...]
    if (...) then GoTo exitMe
    [...]

    if (...) then
        retVal = [some other value]
        GoTo exitMe
    End If

    retVal = [yet another value]
exitMe:
    foo = retVal
    [Code to run when the function ends]
```

```
End Function
```

Of course, this is an absolute personal choice, but don't be surprised to see such a variable in (practically all!) my functions.

1.13. Indenting, Spacing, Commenting

Too often forgotten or under-evaluated, **indenting** is not important, it is *fundamental*. OK, VBA is not Python, where indenting is part of the language syntax. Nonetheless, readability is a basic requirement for all programming languages, and indenting plays an incredibly important role in this regard.

Also, line **spacing** is important to visually divide the code into logical sections. The human eye is extremely capable when it comes to recognizing structures, particularly when they are organized in "blocks." Again, it's all about readability and easiness of modification.

The importance of **commenting** will never be highlighted enough, not only for those who do not know the code and need some explanation but for the code author himself, because I challenge any programmer to go back to a code written months before and remember/understand every single choice made at that time.

In a perfect world, every single line of code should have a comment. Of course, this is not always possible (many times not even needed), but for sure, the more comments you write, the better. A comment should clarify what the variable/line/code section does and its relationship with other variables/lines/code sections. Sometimes, it may be useful to add some markers to specific lines (pretty much what I did before, talking about the function exit points, inserting those 1, 2, and 3 in the code) and mention those markers in the comment.

Let's see this all together. Consider this dummy function:

```
Sub Indentation()
Dim value1 As Integer
Dim value2 As Integer
Dim result As Integer
value1 = InputBox("Enter the first value:")
value2 = InputBox("Enter the second value:")
```

```
If (value1 > 0) Then
result = value1 * 2
If (value2 > 0) Then
result = result + value2
Else
result = result - (value2 / 2)
End If
Else
result = value1 + value2
If (value2 < 0) Then
result = result * value2
End If
End If
MsgBox "The final result is: " & result
End Sub
```

No indentation, no spacing, no comments. The code is hardly comprehensible, and it takes some effort to understand what it does.

Let's add some indentation:

```
Sub Indentation()
Dim value1 As Integer
Dim value2 As Integer
Dim result As Integer
    value1 = InputBox("Enter the first value:")
    value2 = InputBox("Enter the second value:")
    If (value1 > 0) Then
        result = value1 * 2
        If (value2 > 0) Then
            result = result + value2
        Else
            result = result - (value2 / 2)
        End If
```

```
    Else
        result = value1 + value2
        If (value2 < 0) Then
            result = result * value2
        End If
    End If
    MsgBox "The final result is: " & result
End Sub
```

This time, it may still be difficult to follow the logic and understand what this function does, but at least, the blocks that make up the code are clear. It's easy to understand where each If block ends and which its associated Else is.

Now, let's visually separate the logical blocks:

```
Sub Indentation()
Dim value1 As Integer
Dim value2 As Integer
Dim result As Integer

    value1 = InputBox("Enter the first value:")
    value2 = InputBox("Enter the second value:")

    If (value1 > 0) Then
        result = value1 * 2                 ' 1

        If (value2 > 0) Then
            result = result + value2
        Else
            result = result - (value2 / 2)
        End If

    Else
        result = value1 + value2            ' 2
```

```
    If (value2 < 0) Then
        result = result * value2
    End If

  End If

  MsgBox "The final result is: " & result

End Sub
```

Now the eye can visually recognize the blocks that make up the code, and it's easier to understand its structure. This is the most subjective part of the process because we all perceive this information in different ways. Some may find it easier to add a blank line BEFORE line 1 and maybe get rid of the blank line after it (same with line 2) or any other pattern. But whatever the personal choices, the overall readability is certainly improved.

Yet, we may not understand the logic behind the code. And here is where comments play their fundamental role.

Let's add some:

```
Sub Indentation()
Dim value1 As Integer
Dim value2 As Integer
Dim result As Integer

  ' ============================
  ' Get values from user
  ' ============================
  value1 = InputBox("Enter the first value:")
  value2 = InputBox("Enter the second value:")

  ' ============================
  ' Perform calculations
  ' ============================
  If (value1 > 0) Then
```

```
' ------------------------------------------------
' First value >0
' ------------------------------------------------
' We need to double it, because [blah blah blah]
result = value1 * 2

If (value2 > 0) Then
    ' Second value also greater than 0
    ' Add it to the result without modifications
    result = result + value2
Else
    ' Second value <=0
    ' Only add half of it to the result, because [blah
      blah blah]
    result = result - (value2 / 2)
End If

Else
    ' ------------------------------------------------
    ' First value <=0
    ' ------------------------------------------------
    ' Add both values, because [blah blah blah]
    result = value1 + value2

    If (value2 < 0) Then
        ' Second value is negative
        ' Multiply by the result, because [blah blah blah]
        result = result * value2
    End If

End If
```

```
'   ==============================
'   Display the result
'   ==============================
    MsgBox "The final result is: " & result
End Sub
```

Now everything should be clear. Each line/section has an explanation, even though brief and concise, which nonetheless helps the reader understand the logic behind the calculations. Also, note how the use of "graphical" comments (repetitions of = and -) provides an additional visual aid to help the reader separate the code into logical blocks. Of course, other characters can be used (e.g., *), and you may invent more "tricks" to make things even clearer, but this is up to your ingenuity.

So, indent, space, and comment. Indent, space, and comment. Repeat.

1.14. Object Destruction

"Garbage collection" is the operation a system performs to reclaim all the memory that was in use and isn't anymore. For example, when you create an object using the Set instruction, such as in

```
Set obj = New someObject
```

the variable obj occupies one or more memory locations. When obj is not used anymore (e.g., when the function in which it's declared ends), the system *should* release the associated memory to make it available for other variables. It turns out that sometimes this mechanism doesn't work perfectly, so to say (there are technical reasons that are definitely out of scope here[2]). The result is that, in time, an annoying application crash

---

[2] If you are interested in the Garbage Collection details (and complexity), this page may give you a good overview of the whole process: https://learn.microsoft.com/en-us/dotnet/standard/garbage-collection/fundamentals.

might happen, either at developing time or run time. If you are lucky, you will just lose all the latest modifications, but in the worst-case scenario, the whole Access file may get corrupted, and *that* can be a serious issue. But there is an easy solution: just make sure every Set is paired, when the object is not needed anymore, with a

```
Set obj = Nothing
```

Explicitly releasing the memory solves every possible problem related to the memory occupancy.

To be honest, I don't know if this is still a problem. Microsoft states that their Garbage Collector works well, and I have faith that is definitely and absolutely true. Yet, until a few years ago, I experienced this kind of crash, which stopped when I started releasing the memory explicitly and systematically. So, probably, the problem has been totally solved with the last releases, but why risk it? I kept this habit.

1.15. Wall of Declarations

Another controversial topic. *Wall of declaration* or *in-line declarations*? Let's see the difference.

This is an example of wall of declaration:

```
Sub someName()
Dim processNdx As Integer
Dim nextNodeKey As String
Dim oldID As Long, oldKey As String, isNew As Boolean
Dim isDeleted As Boolean
Dim isKilled As Boolean, isRecalled As Boolean, isBlueprint
As Boolean
Dim newID As Long, newKey As String
Dim i As Integer, n As Integer, j As Integer, k As Integer
Dim rs As ADODB.Recordset
```

```
Dim allProdIDs As String, callType As String
Dim itms, itm
Dim parentNdx As Integer, thisNdx As Integer, otherNdx
As Integer
Dim txt As String
[... some code here...]
End Sub
```

And this is how the code looks like when the same variables are declared "in-line":

```
Sub someName()
Dim processNdx As Integer
Dim nextNodeKey As String

[... some code here...]

Dim oldID As Long, oldKey As String, isNew As Boolean
[... some code here...]

Dim isDeleted As Boolean, isKilled As Boolean
[... some code here...]

Dim isRecalled As Boolean, isBlueprint As Boolean
[... some code here...]

Dim newID As Long, newKey As String
[... some code here...]

Dim i As Integer, n As Integer, j As Integer, k As Integer
Dim rs As ADODB.Recordset
[... some code here...]

[... and so on...]
End Sub
```

In a nutshell, with the wall of declarations, all variables are declared at the top of the function. With the in-line approach, every variable is declared within the body of the function, when needed.

Choosing one method or the other is clearly a very personal choice. I know I'm going against the tide here, but I prefer the wall, absolutely no doubt whatsoever. And that is for several reasons:

- I always know where to look, whenever I need to check for a specific variable type or to remove a variable. I do not have to go through the whole code looking for the Dim I need.

- When I go through the code to check it, or to edit it, or to follow the flow, or for any other reason, I find that stumbling into one or more Dim lines is terribly annoying, distracting, and irritating. It disrupts my concentration because I have to stop, note the new variable, maybe ask myself what it is for, etc.

- It's easier to check for unused variables. When you write code, you continuously create and delete variables. If their declarations are drowned in the code, some useless variables may be left behind. Nothing bad, of course, an unused declaration doesn't cause any harm. But when someone else reads your code and finds a variable that is declared and not immediately used, some questions arise. Why is it declared here? Is it a "leftover" of a previous editing and can be deleted, or is it actually used later in the function? If so, again, why is it declared here? You have to spend time checking the rest of the function for an instance of this variable. A simple *Find* may not be enough, in certain situations. And, in any case, it conveys a sense of superficiality.

- Given the previous tip about destructing every object you create, it's immensely easier to check which are the objects involved in your function, for which you need a `set ... = nothing`. They're all named there at the top, and (again) you do not have to check the whole code to find them.

- Since the editor window can be split, it's extremely handy to have the declaration section at the top of the function: all the variables are visible and accessible in the upper half of the screen, while I write my code in the bottom half.

In other words, "the wall" can be accessed much quicker to add, delete, modify, search, and check my variable types and names.

1.16. Dim ... As New

When you handle an object, you may declare it like this:

```
Dim obj As New objType
```

But I definitely prefer to use this second version:

```
Dim obj As objType
Set obj = New objType
```

There are several good reasons why I prefer this "verbose" alternative:

- With the `As New` version, the object is automatically created the first time it's *referenced* (not when it's *declared*), if it doesn't exist already. This means that every time the object name is found in the code, Access must check whether it already exists or not.

So, every access to the object has an implied If obj Is Nothing Then Set obj = New objType in front of it, and this is a waste of time. OK, we're talking about nanoseconds, yet...

- It gives me more control on the creation and the destruction of the object.

- The As New version may lead to unwanted results. Consider this fragment of code:

```
Dim obj as New SomeObject

[...]

set obj = Nothing           ' Make sure object
                                doesn't exist

If (obj Is Nothing) Then    ' Referencing the object

                            '  implicitly creates it...

    MsgBox "Object destroyed"  ' ...so this is NEVER
                                    executed!

Else

    MsgBox "Object alive"

End If
```

And what about this:

```
Dim obj As New Collection
For x = 1 To 100
    obj.Add...
Next
```

How many collections are created? Well, obviously one, the first time the object is referenced, in the first loop iteration (x=1). Let's say that 20 items are added to it. On the second iteration (x=2), the *same* collection is used, so every new item is added to the previous 20. Is it really what you wanted? Or did you mean to create a new collection on every iteration? Even though this may be absolutely clear in your mind, it may be rather confusing for anyone else. The explicit creation of a collection when you need it sweeps away any ambiguity.

1.17. Make Variant Explicit

We all know that when you Dim a variable without specifying the data type, Access assumes that variable is a Variant. And even though this is absolutely acceptable, I consider this a bad style of programming because whoever reads the code doesn't know what you were thinking when you wrote it. Was it actually meant to be a Variant? Or you simply forgot to specify the correct data type? This doubt may force the poor guy to check all your code trying to understand which of the two options is correct to make sure there won't be any error at run time. Remember, write your code as if whoever replaces you is a psycho killer...

1.18. Boolean and Date Data Type

Boolean is a weird data type, let's face it. A Boolean is defined to be False or True, but the first value translates internally into a 0 and the second into a −1, which are actually Integer values (not even Byte because of the minus sign).

Now, there is nothing wrong with using the type Boolean in your applications, but I had to face a huge amount of problems every time I had to convert my code to other languages or to migrate to other platforms. For example, if you have to move your back end to SQL Server, there is no

Boolean there but a BIT data type that only accepts Null, 0, and 1. Oracle doesn't even support anything similar, so if you have to port your database to Oracle, you will have to change several things in the tables and in the code. Obviously, this may not be a problem at all, and as long as you stay with Access, using Boolean is perfectly fine. But if there is even a vague chance that in a future you may need to switch to another platform, then it's extremely more convenient to use an Integer value, with 0 as False and 1 as True.

Of course, in the code, you will have to write your conditions like

```
If (varName = 1) Then
```

and no longer as

```
If (varName) Then
```

or

```
If (varName = True) Then
```

But in my experience, I have found that this is a small price to pay in cases like those I mentioned.

The same goes with Date. I hate the Date data type, to be honest. It's hard to handle, subject to localization problems – day, month, year or month, day, year? Internally, a date is always expected in the American format, but in the code? And in the form controls or the queries? Null values, too, are hideous and cause subtle errors and problems. And just like before, porting your tables and your code to other machines or platforms may cause all sort of problems. I really do not like dates.

What I normally do is replacing all Date with Long. It works because internally dates are stored as Long anyway. No more Null to worry about, no more format problems and ambiguity, easy sorting, easy comparisons (now they are numbers!), total portability to other machines and platforms with no modifications. There is one drawback only: you must use CDate() to see the actual date. For example, a number like 44656 doesn't tell much.

We have to use `CDate(44656)` to know that it means "05/04/2022" or 5th April 2022. Well, for me, and for some of you. But an American would read this as May 4th because dates *do* generate these kinds of problems. But I think using `CDate()` is, again, a very small price to pay, compared to the advantages of handling numbers instead of dates.

And if we need the time, also? Well, use a `Double`, not a `Long`. The integer part is still the date, and the decimal part is the time. Again, we'll need `CDate()` (on the whole number or on the two parts separately), but I believe the benefits outweigh the drawbacks.

1.19. SELECT CASE

Usually, we use `If` when we need a two-way decision (sometimes three or even four) and `SELECT CASE` when the options are more. Sometimes, though, I find that a `SELECT CASE` has some additional advantages, even when the options are only two. For example:

```
Sub Test()
   If (V1 = val1) Then
      [some code here]
   Else
      [more code here]
   End If
End Sub
```

is perfectly fine, but the `ELSE` part doesn't make it really clear as to which is the option that makes it happen. Is it any value, like in (`V1 <> val1`)? Is it a specific value, say, (`V1 = val2`)? Sometimes I prefer the following:

```
Sub Test()
   Select Case V1
      Case val1
```

```
        [some code here]
    Case val2
        [more code here]
    End Select
End Sub
```

In this case I exactly know what values I am expecting for V1, which is extremely useful when debugging, and it's super clear which part of the code is executed in either case. It's also very easy to add more branches in case, while developing, I realize that V1 may assume more than two values.

The same works when the Else part should be executed whenever *any* value different from val1 occurs:

```
Sub Test()
    Select Case V1
        Case val1
            [some code here]
        Case Else
            [more code here]
    End Select
End Sub
```

In other cases, SELECT can help increase the code readability. Consider this situation. You have two variables, V1 and V2, each of which picks values in a discrete set, say, (val1, val2, val3). You have to check for all possible combinations. Would you go for a cascading If?

```
Sub Test()
    If (V1 = val1) Then
        If (V2 = val1) Then
        ElseIf (V2 = val2) Then
        ElseIf (V2 = val3) Then
        End If
```

```
    ElseIf (V1 = val2) Then
        If (V2 = val1) Then
        ElseIf (V2 = val2) Then
        ElseIf (V2 = val3) Then
        End If
    ElseIf (V1 = val3) Then
        If (V2 = val1) Then
        ElseIf (V2 = val2) Then
        ElseIf (V2 = val3) Then
        End If
    End If
End Sub
```

Not quite readable, I would say, particularly if the code in the different branches is long. Consider this solution instead:

```
Sub Test()
    Select Case V1 & "@" & V2
        Case val1 & "@" & val1
        Case val1 & "@" & val2
        Case val1 & "@" & val3
        Case val2 & "@" & val1
        Case val2 & "@" & val2
        Case val2 & "@" & val3
        Case val3 & "@" & val1
        Case val3 & "@" & val2
        Case val3 & "@" & val3
        End Select
End Sub
```

Not only is this more compact, but at the start of every branch, it's always clear which values for V1 and V2 you are evaluating. Adding the "unlikely" character @ makes sure that there is no possible overlap between the couple of values. Consider, for example, what happens when `val1 = 123` and `val2 = 45` or `val1 = 12` and `val2 = 345`. The simple concatenation `val1 & val2` would return 12345 in both cases. With the @ character, we would have 123@45 in the first case and 12@345 in the second.

Of course, if @ is a character that *may* occur in your value set, a different "unlikely" character must be chosen: for example, §, or ^, or |, or ~, and so on. In those rare cases where *all* characters can be present, you can go with the good old unprintable character `Chr$(0)`.

1.20. Call Instruction

Many programmers like to use it. If they have a function called `myFunc(parm1, parm2)`, they invoke it as

```
Call myFunc(a, b)
```

I don't really get it. The same line can be written as

```
myFunc a,b
```

which I think is simpler, more concise, and more readable. Some say that using `Call` makes it clearer to the reader that a function is being called, but if readers need this kind of hint, and they don't understand that `myFunc` here IS a call to a function, they probably shouldn't spend their time on VBA.

There's also another reason. Try this code:

```
[CODE MODULE]

Option Explicit

Public Sub Test()
Dim a As Variant

   a = 2
   Test2 a

End Sub

Private Sub Test2(parm1 As Integer)
   Debug.Print parm1 * 2
End Sub
```

Here, the function Test() calls a second function, Test2(), which does something with the passed parameter. When you run it, you'll get an error because you are passing a Variant to a function expecting an Integer. You can solve this problem in either of two ways:

- Use ByVal in Test2 signature:

   ```
   Private Sub Test2(ByVal parm1 As Integer)
   ```

- Enclose a in parentheses:

   ```
   Test2 (a)
   ```

Both are valid ways to pass a parameter ByVal and not ByRef (which is the default). If you use the Call keyword and you don't want to use the first method, you should write

```
Call Test2((a))
```

and I think this is uselessly hard to read and to justify since `Test2 (a)` is much, much simpler.

1.21. Feedback

A cursor changes to a hand when it hovers over a clickable object or to an hourglass when an operation is ongoing. A button, or a menu item, gets disabled if it's not useful/applicable in that specific moment. A progress bar is shown during a time-consuming operation. A label shows a total of a list of rows. A message box pops up when a long operation ends. And the text in the box explains what has been done, if there's an error, and how to solve it. These are all examples of "feedback," that is, communication with the user. Never leave your users in doubt about what they have to do, what's going on, which operations are legal and which are not, and what the results of their actions are.

Giving the user visual and/or informative types of feedback like these is definitely an extremely good programming practice that increases usability and improves the so-called user experience. Besides, disabling controls when they are not needed may provide some degree of protection against weird errors that may happen if we let the user choose an operation that is not allowed at that moment.

1.22. Conclusion

As I said when I started, by no means these are meant to be "best" practices. These are just my "favorite" practices and techniques, which you may agree upon or contemptuously reject – you have full right to do that. I just hope that some of you may have found some useful input. But again, whatever your style choices, always be consistent. I'll do the same, so in the rest of the book, these are the practices I'm going to follow and apply.

In the next section, we are going to face one of the most powerful tools an object-oriented programming (OOP) language can offer: classes. Yes, I know there are some objections against considering VBA a real OOP language. And, really, it's *not*. But even so, its limited OOP capabilities will be more than enough to build intriguing, funny, colorful, unusual interfaces, as we are going to find out in the third section of this book.

CHAPTER 2

VBA Classes

…where the basics of VBA classes are discussed.

The importance of mastering classes should be obvious in any OOP programming language. Knowing how to build and use them is crucial because it enables you to create organized, reusable, and efficient code. Classes provide a blueprint for creating objects, promoting code modularity and encapsulation. This empowers you to build complex systems and enhance code readability and maintainability while facilitating teamwork and code collaboration.

Now, what exactly are OOP languages, and why is VBA not one of them? The OOP (object-oriented programming) is a programming paradigm that utilizes the concept of "objects" to structure and design computer programs. In this context, a class is a template defining the attributes (data) and behaviors (methods/functions) shared by objects of that class, and an object is an instance of that template. We'll see some examples in a moment.

The key principles of an OOP language include

1. **Encapsulation**: Data and methods are bundled together, hiding the internal implementation details from the users.

2. **Abstraction**: The user can focus on the object's essential characteristics and behaviors since a class hides all unnecessary complexities, making it easier to understand and use the objects.

© The Editor(s) (if applicable) and The Author(s),
under exclusive license to APress Media, LLC, part of Springer Nature 2024
A. Grimaldi, *Advanced interactive interfaces with Access*,
https://doi.org/10.1007/979-8-8688-0808-1_2

3. **Inheritance**: Allowing classes to inherit attributes and methods from other classes, promoting code reuse and hierarchical relationships.

4. **Polymorphism**: Objects of different classes can be treated as instances of a common superclass, enabling flexibility and dynamic behavior.

Languages like Java, C++, Python, and C# are examples of popular OOP languages, as they fully embrace the principles and concepts of object-oriented programming.

What's wrong with VBA, then? Well, VBA is often considered a "light" or "limited" OOP language, for it does support some OOP features, but it lacks some advanced capabilities found in more modern and fully-fledged OOP languages.

VBA does have elements of OOP, such as follows:

- **Classes and objects**: VBA allows you to define classes and create objects based on those classes.

- **Encapsulation**: You can use private variables and properties to encapsulate data within a class.

- **Inheritance**: VBA supports single-level inheritance, where one class can inherit from another.

However, there are limitations in VBA that distinguish it from more advanced OOP languages:

- **No multiple inheritance**: VBA does not support multiple inheritance, where a class can inherit from multiple base classes.

- **No abstract classes**: VBA does not have abstract classes, which are common in traditional OOP languages.

44

- **Limited polymorphism**: VBA's polymorphism is less flexible compared to languages like Java or C++. Polymorphism in VBA is primarily achieved using the Variant data type.

- **Limited support for inheritance modifiers**: VBA does not provide keywords like `Protected` or `Internal`, limiting the control over accessibility for inherited members.

Due to these limitations (and to a diffused, generalized, absolutely unjustified aversion to this language[1]), VBA is often seen as a procedural language with some OOP features rather than a fully-fledged OOP language. The good news is that we can happily live with these limitations (and sometimes *exploit* them, as we'll see later), and classes remain a powerful tool to create our complex applications.

I assume that if you are reading this book, you already know something about classes. Maybe you're not an expert, but you should know how to work with them (at least in theory). But, to stay on the safe side, I am going for a quick recap of the main concepts, just to make sure we're all on the same page. We'll use an easy and oversimplified example. The typical example you can find in all dedicated books is "a car" or "an animal." But they're too obvious and too easy, so we're going to model something less tangible like a "meeting."

---

[1] I have my personal opinion about this generalized dislike. First of all, VBA is easy to learn, and "easy" is often perceived as "not powerful enough." Second, there's not much money involved when it comes to VBA. If you have an MS Office license and a good VBA programmer, you've got everything you need. There's no additional license, maintenance or service contract, complementary environment, technical support, external company, and such. It's just an extremely cheap programming language, and it doesn't move money around. It's a cynical thought, I admit it, but I do think there's some truth in it.

2.1. Creating a Class

Creating a class is extremely easy: in the Code window (Alt+F11), click the `Insert Module` button and select Class Module (Figure 2-1).

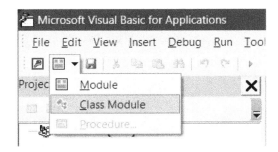

Figure 2-1. *Creating a class module*

It's a good thing to save the project right now and give the class a meaningful name – which, of course, depends on what you are trying to do with it. In our case, I'd say that `clsMeeting` would be a very good choice. In the following, this box will represent a code module:

CLSMEETING

Let's agree on a convention: from now on, to save some space, I will mainly show the new code only, not ALL the code. An ellipsis (`[...]`) may replace the previously written code, and all new code will be marked in **bold**.

2.2. Instantiating a Class

Remember that a class is not a "usable" object. A class is just a blueprint from which objects ("instances") are generated. To "instantiate" a class means to create an instance of that class, to create an object that contains all the properties and methods defined in that class. This instantiation can be put in a form module, or in a code module, or even within another class, as we're going to see in a moment.

If you want your instance to be global to the application, you'll probably use something like this in a code module:

```
[CODE MODULE]
```

```
Public Meeting As clsMeeting

Public Sub initApp()
  set Meeting = New clsMeeting

  [Other code needed when the application starts]
End Sub
```

Then you can use any form (probably the first form to be loaded) to call initApp(), and the class instance will be created and made available throughout the whole application.

```
[FORM MODULE]
```

```
Private Sub Form_Load()
  initApp()

End Sub
```

Sometimes, though, you may want your instance to be only used within a single form. In this case, you can declare and create it in the form module itself:

```
[FORM MODULE]

Private Meeting As clsMeeting

Private Sub Form_Load()
  Set Meeting = New clsMeeting
End Sub
```

If this is the case, and if closing the form won't also quit the application, you may also want to use the Form_Close() (or Form_Unload()) to destroy the instance (remember what we said about the garbage collection?):

```
[FORM MODULE]

Private Meeting As clsMeeting

Private Sub Form_Load()
  Set Meeting = New clsMeeting
End Sub

Private Sub Form_Close()
  Set Meeting = Nothing
End Sub
```

2.3. Properties

So, how do we model a meeting with a class? Let's start with the properties. What can the properties of a meeting be? Well, subject, date, time, and duration sound a reasonable starting set:

CLSMEETING

```
Option Explicit

Private Type recLocals
  Subject As String
  Date As Long
  Time As Double
  Duration As Integer
End Type
Private Locals As recLocals
```

As you can see, I'm here using my usual style and conventions, as discussed previously: a UDT named recLocals, a Date of type Long, a Time of type Double, all embedded into a variable named Locals (of type recLocals). Also note that we can use VBA reserved words (Date and Time) because VBA can tell a reserved word from a variable within a UDT.

Again, many people may tell you that this naming convention sucks because every local variable name *must* be prefixed with m (or m_), which means "module," *because it's a local variable* – something like mSubject, mDuration, or maybe m_Locals. And again, I don't care. That may be true with a normal Dim declaration, but using a UDT changes the game. Here, the main variable is named Locals, which is (duh!) rather self-explanatory, and its internal variables are... *internal*, so they're clearly *local* as well. I don't feel there's any need for additional, redundant, useless characters. Do I have to call it udtLocals? No, I know it's a UDT and don't need to be reminded every time I see it.

Now, the object properties are usually accessible to the users. In our example, the users will need to manipulate them all, so we have to give them a way to assign values and to read the current values.

Probably the first solution that pops up in our minds is that both the UDT and `Locals` can be declared `Public` so that users can access each of the variables. Well, no. *Absolutely no.* That's really a terrible idea. If we give the users the power to change the class variables directly, they can enter any value they want with no control at all, and anything could happen: we would totally lose control of the input, the output, and all that happens in the middle. A horrible scenario. And for the structure that won't even work. If you replace `Private Type recLocals` with `Public Type recLocals`, the debugger will raise the error shown in Figure 2-2.

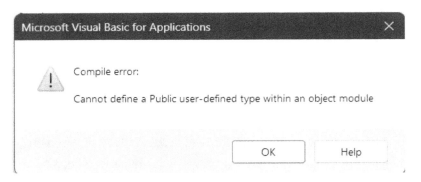

Figure 2-2. *Can't create a Public structure in a class*

You are not allowed to create a `Public` structure within a class. If you think about it, it makes some sense. If the structure is to be used by the class only, it doesn't need to be public. But if it has to be used by other components of the application, then it shouldn't be provided by the class, which by definition is a totally "passive" object until the moment an instance is created. If a public structure was declared in a class, it would be available to other modules even if no instance of the class is created, which defeats the OOP concept of a class as an isolated object[2]. We'll see in a moment how we can bypass this limitation, but for now, just surrender: the structure must remain `Private`.

So, how can we allow the user to set and read the variables? We can write *properties*. By encapsulating the code in controlled routines, we are free to perform all the necessary checks, calculations, and whatever it takes to make sure we can safely assign or retrieve a value.

A class property can be one of three types: LET, GET, or SET.

- **LET properties**

    A LET property is used to assign a value to a variable:

CLSMEETING

```
Public Property Let meetingDate(dt As Long)
  [Checks on dt if needed]
  Locals.Date = dt
End Property
```

As you can see, it's marked as `Public`, so it's visible from "outside" the class module. In this case, it takes a single parameter (a `Long` instead of a `Date`, as we discussed previously), runs all necessary checks and operations on it, and then assigns this value to the local variable `Locals.Date`. Also note that in this case, we can't name the property `Date()`: VBA would throw a syntax error because `Date` is a VBA reserved word and can't be used as a custom function name.

---

[2] The question may arise: "How come I can't declare a public structure, but I can declare a public variable?" The answer should be obvious, though: they are totally different entities. A variable is something you can assign a value to, and a class exposing a variable makes sense (though it should be avoided as much as possible). A UDT is just the description of a data structure and can't be assigned any value *per se*.

- **GET properties**

  A GET property is the complement for the LET property: it retrieves a variable value and returns it:

CLSMEETING

```
Public Property Get meetingDate() As Long
  meetingDate = Locals.Date
End Property
```

There are just two rules:[3]

- It must have the same name of the corresponding LET property (in this case, meetingDate).

- Its return value type must match the LET property's parameter type (in this case, Long).

Let's add all the properties we need to handle the other pieces of information:

CLSMEETING

```
Public Property Let Subject(meetingSubject As String)
  Locals.Subject = meetingSubject
End Property

Public Property Get Subject() As String
  Subject = Locals.Subject
End Property
```

---

[3] Actually, there would be something more to say especially about the number of parameters, but this is not meant to be a full course about classes...

```
Public Property Get meetingTime() As Double
  meetingTime = Locals.Time
End Property

Public Property Let meetingTime(tm As Double)
  Locals.Time = tm
End Property

Public Property Get Duration() As Integer
  Duration = Locals.Duration
End Property

Public Property Let Duration(d As Integer)
  Locals.Duration = d
End Property
```

- **SET properties**

    A SET property is used to set an object value. We won't need it in our meeting example, but this is how it should look like:

    ```
    Public Property Set myObject(obj As Object)
        Set localObject = obj
    End Property
    ```

    To retrieve the object, we can use a normal GET property, respecting the preceding rules:

    ```
    Public Property Get myObject() As Object
        Set myObject = localObject
    End Property
    ```

In these examples, we only entered one line of code in each property, but of course, they can be considered as normal subs/functions, so they can contain all the code they need.

The users of your class will not have access to all this code: they will simply invoke the property they need. For example, having created the Meeting instance as shown previously, to handle the meeting date, they may write (in a form or in a code module)

```
Sub someProcedure()
   [...]
   Meeting.Date = #6 Aug 2024#      ' Let
   MsgBox CDate(Meeting.Date)       ' Get
   [...]
End Sub
```

The first statement invokes the LET version of the property meetingDate to assign a value to the date. The second statement triggers the GET version, which returns the value.

2.4. Methods

"Methods" is a name that embraces all the public subs and functions the class provides to the users. They are nothing more than normal public subs/functions, and they follow all the rules that apply to any VBA sub/function.

More often than not, there is no *functional* difference between a property and a method/function. For example, the meetingDate (LET) property we wrote before can also be written as a method:

```
Public Sub meetingDate(dt As Long)
   Locals.Date = dt
End Sub
```

It works as well. As a rule of thumb, if you need to set and retrieve a property value, a LET/GET couple is a better and more logical choice, also because they have the same name, undoubtedly a more elegant solution than using two separate methods (e.g., `setMeetingDate()` and `getMeetingDate()`). Otherwise, generally speaking, using a method/function or a property is totally up to you. There's obviously a difference from the users' point of view, in the way they call it. For the property, they would have to write

```
Meeting.meetingDate = #6 Aug 2024#
```

as seen before. For the method, they would have to write

```
Meeting.setMeetingDate #6 Aug 2024#
```

2.5. "Companion" Module

Now, say that we want to add some invitees to our meeting. An "invitee" has several properties such as name, mail, and response status (unknown, accepted, declined, or tentative), but we can also imagine adding some methods (e.g., `sendEmail()`, `Remove()`, `Hide()`, etc.). Properties and methods: this means a class. Let's create a class, then, and name it `clsInvitees`:

```
                        CLSMEETING

Option Explicit
```

Since we have to add several invitees, an array may be a good structure to hold them all. But what would the data type be for this array? It can't be a single string: as we said, for each invitee, we need several pieces of information. And whenever we need several pieces of information about a single entity, a UDT is probably the best choice. The problem is that, presumably, this UDT must also be available to other components of our application: for example, there must be a form allowing the users to add or delete invitees to the meeting. In a word, it must be `Public`.

And here comes the problem: we can't create a public structure in a class, as we said earlier. Sometimes, though, we need that, like now. Actually, as we're going to see in the next part, it happens quite often that a class needs a structure, which is also needed by other modules. From a formal point of view, this clearly "breaks" the OOP's isolation requirement, but do we really need to be so strict? After all, even some degree of denormalization is acceptable in a database, if it simplifies some operations.[4] We already said that the GoTo statement clashes with the "structured code" paradigm – nonetheless, it's OK to use it if it helps us keep the code under control. So why shouldn't we accept a little exception to this isolation dogma? And after all, VBA detractors say VBA is not an OOP language because it doesn't match all OOP requirements. Well, this is true. Let's use this at our own advantage, then.

What we can do is, I think, a reasonable compromise. We create a code module with the public structure. This module will always be "linked" to the class, so if we need to export the class into another project, we'll also have to export the module. And to mark this strict relation, we'll name the module along the class name.

So, let's add a new module with the public structure and name it `mdlInvitees` after the class:

MDLINVITEES

```
Option Explicit

Public Type recEntry
  Name As String
```

---

[4] Denormalization is the process of optimizing the read performance of a database by adding redundant data. While it can speed up data retrieval, it may lead to increased storage requirements and data inconsistency risks.

```
Mail As String
Status As String
End Type
```

clsInvitees can now use this structure to define its local variable:

CLSINVITEES

```
Option Explicit
```

Private myEntries() As recEntry

Again: this reference to an external object breaks the isolation paradigm. We accept it, but we must be well aware of that.

2.6. Nested Classes

It's logical to declare our invitees within clsMeeting since they are somehow a "property" or an "attribute" of the meeting.

CLSMEETING

```
Option Explicit
```

Public Invitees As clsInvitees   ' 1

```
Private Type recLocals
  [...]
End Type
Private Locals As recLocals
```

57

```vba
Private Sub Class_Initialize()
  Set Invitees = New clsInvitees
End Sub

Private Sub Class_Terminate()
  Set Invitees = Nothing
End Sub
```

This new declaration line (1) is not trivial. We are declaring an instance of a class (clsInvitees), *within* another class (clsMeeting). Basically, we are nesting two classes. Though this may sound a bit strange, this technique can be extremely helpful to better organize the code and the object hierarchy, in case an object is part of another object. The Class_ Initialize() event is then used to actually create the class instance, destroyed as usual when the class terminates.

Let's recap what we have done so far. clsMeeting is the top-level class that models a meeting with its invitees:

CLSMEETING

```vba
Option Explicit

Public Invitees As clsInvitees                    ' 1

Private Type recLocals
  Subject As String
  meetingDate As Long
  meetingTime As Double
  Duration As Integer
End Type
Private Locals As recLocals

[...List of LET/GET properties...]
```

The `Invitees` object (line 1) is an instance of the following (sub-)class:

CLSINVITEES

```
Option Explicit

Private myEntries() As recEntry
```

where all the invitees are packed into an array of structured items, the structure being described in a "companion" code module:

MDLINVITEES

```
Option Explicit

Public Type recEntry
  Name As String
  Mail As String
  Status As String
End Type
```

Now, where do we go from here? Well, we need some more code in `clsInvitees` to have something to work with. First of all, we can use the `Initialize()` event to *dim* the array, which would otherwise remain undefined:

```
┌─────────────────────────────────────────────────────────┐
│                      CLSINVITEES                          │
└─────────────────────────────────────────────────────────┘
```

```
Option Explicit

Private myEntries() As recEntry
```

```
Private Sub Class_Initialize()
  ReDim myEntries(0)
End Sub
```

Then, we're probably going to need a property that returns all the entries:

```
┌─────────────────────────────────────────────────────────┐
│                      CLSINVITEES                          │
└─────────────────────────────────────────────────────────┘
```

```
Option Explicit

[...]
```

```
Public Property Get allEntries() As recEntry()
  allEntries = myEntries
End Property
```

What if the users need one single entry, based on its index in the array? Well, this sounds a redundant feature since they can use the newly created allEntries(), but hey, it's our class. We can write all the properties and all the methods we want. Let's consider it a shortcut for the users:

```
                    CLSINVITEES
```

```
Option Explicit
[...]

Public Property Get Entry(ndx As Integer) As recEntry
  If (ndx>=0) And (ndx <= UBound(myEntries)) Then Entry =
  myEntries(ndx)
End Property
```

And then we need a method to add invitees to the list and to manipulate their data:

```
                    CLSINVITEES
```

```
[...]

Public Function Add(ByVal entryName As String, _
                    ByVal entryMail As String, _
                    ByVal entryStatus As String)
Dim ndx As Integer

  ' Add a new slot to myEntries()
  ndx = UBound(myEntries) + 1
  ReDim Preserve myEntries(ndx)
  With myEntries(ndx)
    .Name = entryName
    .Mail = entryMail
    .Status = entryStatus
  End With

End Function
```

```
Public Property Let entryName(ndx As Integer, nm As String)
  myEntries(ndx).Name = nm
End Property

Public Property Let entryStatus(ndx As Integer, st As String)
  myEntries(ndx).Status = st
End Property
```

[...Other methods/functions/properties as needed...]

I'm not writing all the properties and methods, but this should be enough to understand how it works.

Let's say we wrote all the properties and all the methods we need. How do users use this code? Well, from a code module or from a form, they have to instantiate the class as we saw earlier, and... use them. For example:

[A CODE MODULE]

```
Option Explicit

Public Sub Test()
Dim Meeting As clsMeeting
Dim knt As Integer, i As Integer

  Set Meeting = New clsMeeting

  Meeting.Duration = 15
  Meeting.Subject = "My First Meeting"

  Meeting.Invitees.Add "John Doe", "John.Doe@some.org",
  "Pending"
  Meeting.Invitees.Add "Jane Doe", "Jane.Doe@any.com",
  "Pending"
```

```
  knt = UBound(Meeting.Invitees.allEntries)
  For i = 1 To knt
    With Meeting.Invitees.Entry(i)
      MsgBox .Name & ": " & .Mail & " (" & .Status & ")"
    End With
  Next

  Set Meeting = Nothing
End Sub
```

As you can see while you type, the nested classes are beautifully handled by VBA and its Intellisense engine, generating a nested, easy-to-use structure.

2.7. Conclusion

Don't underestimate classes. I heard many programmers saying they never used classes and never felt the need to use them. I guess that's because they never went past the usual, classic, simple, boring, in-the-box, academic VBA applications. But I still remember very well what I had to do before I learned how to use a class, to handle dozens or more objects on a screen – hundreds of code lines, cloned functions, repeated code, days and nights for debugging and maintenance. Classes literally saved my life and allowed me to create those interactive, graphical interfaces I like so much, with very little effort.

There would be more to say about classes, but we're going to deal with them a lot in the last part of this book. So, leave them for a while, and let's focus our attention to some different topics. It's time to tackle the hard stuff.

CHAPTER 3

The Presence Vector Technique

A powerful yet simple technique to store a large amount of information in a small place.

Before tackling the next tool, the timeline, we unfortunately need some theory. We're going to talk about that nice technique known as "presence vector" or "bit field" or called by many other names, which will be the key to placing objects on the timeline.

A practical example may give you a hint of what this technique is about.

You are a teacher in a classroom and have, say, eight students. You have to keep track of their daily *presence* during the course (hence the name). What would you do? You'd probably set up a structure like this (Figure 3-1):

- A table (Students) with information about the students, such as name and other info

- A table (Lessons) describing each lesson (date, venue, discussed topics, other info)

- A joining table (Presence) to record the attendance data per student per day

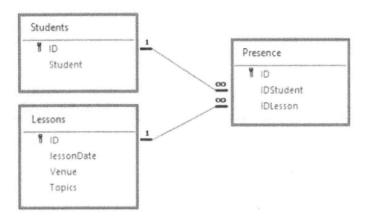

Figure 3-1. *Typical three-table structure*

That's pretty much standard, but it needs

- Three tables

- Two joins

- Three Long fields (4 bytes), which sum up to 12 bytes per record per day per student

If you have eight students and the course goes on for 30 days, you have 8*30*12 = about 3KB of presence information, plus the overhead due to the additional table, the joins, the indexed fields, and so on. And every operation on the presence data takes a three-table query. For example: How do you know who was attending a specific lesson? Probably with something like this:

```
SELECT Students.Student
FROM Lessons INNER JOIN (Students INNER JOIN Presence
ON Students.ID = Presence.IDStudent) ON Lessons.ID = Presence.
IDLesson WHERE (Lessons.lessonDate)=[wantedDate])
```

Well, what if I tell you that `Presence`, with all its links, records, indexes, and all its overhead, is totally useless and can be replaced by a single byte field in `Lessons` and that you can forget about this query?

Let's recall some basic binary concepts.

Every number can be expressed in binary notation (Figure 3-2) that is using 0 and 1 only. How a decimal number can be translated to binary is out of our scope. But we must know how to read a binary number.

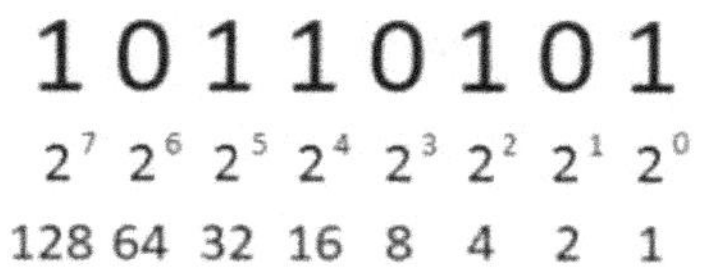

$$1\ 0\ 1\ 1\ 0\ 1\ 0\ 1$$
$$2^7\ 2^6\ 2^5\ 2^4\ 2^3\ 2^2\ 2^1\ 2^0$$
$$128\ 64\ 32\ 16\ 8\ 4\ 2\ 1$$

Figure 3-2. *Binary number*

Each bit represents a power of 2. The rightmost bit (named *bit 0*) is 2^0, that's 1 in decimal. The next one (*bit 1*) is 2^1, 2 in decimal. Then 2^2, that's 4. Then 2^3, that's 8. Then 2^4, that's 16, and so on.

To know what a binary number is in decimal, just add the values of the bits that are set to 1. For example, 10110101 is $2^0 + 2^2 + 2^4 + 2^5 + 2^7 = 181$. There's actually a quicker method, but I'll show you how it works at the end of this discussion, so now we can focus on the main topic.

So far so good, and we can also define sum, subtraction, multiplication, and division. But in this context, the most interesting thing is that we can perform *logical bitwise* operations, that is to say, AND, OR, XOR, and NOT.

AND				The AND between two bits is 1 if and only if both bits are 1. You can think of an AND as if it was a multiplication.
0	0	1	1	
0	1	0	1	
0	0	0	1	

OR				An OR between two bits is 1 if at least one bit is 1. It's not exactly an addition, but it's close.
0	0	1	1	
0	1	0	1	
0	1	1	1	

XOR				The XOR, or "eXclusive OR," is like the OR, but a bit more restrictive. It gives 1 if either one or the other bit is 1, but not both, in which case it returns a 0.
0	0	1	1	
0	1	0	1	
0	1	1	0	

NOT		Finally, the NOT operation, which is very easy as it just flips a 0 into 1 and a 1 into 0.
0	1	
1	0	

You need to understand and remember these four tables, which are the foundation for every logical operation on binary numbers.

So, where do we go with this stuff? Here's the trick. Since we have eight students, we take a single byte (that's to say 8 bits) for every lesson day and assign one bit to each of our students, as shown in Figure 3-3.

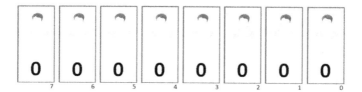

Figure 3-3. *Assigning the bits*

The rightmost bit, bit 0, is assigned to Student 1. The next bit, bit 1, is assigned to Student 2, and so on. The leftmost bit, bit 7, is assigned to Student 8. Now, we can say that if a student was attending that specific lesson, the correspondent bit would be 1. If the student missed the lesson, the bit would be 0. This way, all the students' presence on one specific day can be stored in one single byte. Figure 3-4 shows an example, where the (byte) number 237 represents all presences in a single day of lesson.

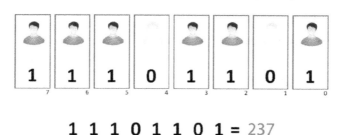

$$1\ 1\ 1\ 0\ 1\ 1\ 0\ 1 = 237$$

Figure 3-4. *Bit vector example*

In our cases, 8 students × 30 days × 1 byte is about 240 bytes, a reduction of about 93% in terms of storing space, compared to the three-table structure. Not to mention the third table overhead that's now gone with its two joins, indexes, and such. And forget the three-table query; we're going to see how easy it is to check and modify this information using our logical functions. For this, we need to introduce the concept of *mask*.

A mask is a number that uniquely identifies one or more bits within a byte. But we already met these guys, a moment ago (Figure 3-5): Bit 0 is 2^0, which is 1. Bit 1 is 2^1, which is 2. Then 2^2, which is 4, and so on.

$$1\ 0\ 1\ 1\ 0\ 1\ 0\ 1$$

$$2^7\ 2^6\ 2^5\ 2^4\ 2^3\ 2^2\ 2^1\ 2^0$$

$$128\ 64\ 32\ 16\ 8\ 4\ 2\ 1$$

Figure 3-5. *Binary masks*

These are all *masks* because each of these numbers uniquely identifies a specific bit.

We can also use combinations of these values: for example, $2^1 + 2^5 = 2 + 32 = 34$ is a mask that identifies bit 1 and bit 5, and it's easy to see that there is no other possible combination that gives the same value, so 34 is unique for these two bits.

Now, let's start with an empty vector V. Keep in mind that a *vector* in this context is a number (a byte, in this case), whose 8 bits (in this case) represent our eight students. "Empty" here means its value is 0. Let's see how we can perform all the operations we may need:

1. *Set a bit to 1 (a student is attending the lesson)*

    If you remember the OR table, that's extremely easy. For example, if we want to turn bit 5 on, we can use its mask:

Binary		Decimal	
0 0 0 0 0 0 0 0	OR	0	OR
0 0 1 0 0 0 0 0		32	
0 0 1 0 0 0 0 0		32	

Here, we see the same operation in binary and in decimal. The current value of the vector is ORed with the proper mask for the involved bit, and the result is a number with that bit on. Note that this works regardless of the starting value for that bit: in this case, the starting value for bit 5 is 0, but if it was 1, the result would have been the same because that's how the OR works. So, the operation we need to turn a bit on is just:

```
V OR mask
```

2. *Check if a student was attending a specific lesson*

   This is the equivalent of the old three-table query. We basically need to know whether the student's bit is on or off. Again, if you remember how the AND works, this is quite straightforward. For example, for Student 6:

Binary	Decimal
1 0 1 0 1 1 1 0 AND	174 AND
0 0 1 0 0 0 0 0	32
0 0 1 0 0 0 0 0	32

We AND our vector (whatever its current value) with the student's mask, and if the bit is 1, we get a nonzero result. More precisely, since all the other bits are turned off by the AND with a 0, Vector AND mask is either equal to mask (32 in our example) if the bit we're checking is on or equal to 0 if it's off. So, a simple AND is enough to replace our three-table query:

```
(V AND Mask) > 0
```

3. *Set a bit to 0*

Someone asks us to make sure Student 5 is considered as "not present" for a specific lesson. This means we must make sure that the student's bit in that lesson's vector is 0, while leaving the other bits untouched. This is going to be a bit harder because we may not know the current status of that specific bit: is it on or already off? We just need to perform a "blind update," so to say, to make sure it's off.

Let's consider the two cases separately. First, suppose bit 4 is on. We want to turn it off, ONLY that bit. We can't use an AND or an OR, as they would affect all the other bits as well. An XOR seems to be more useful:

Binary	Decimal
1 1 0 1 0 1 1 1 XOR	215 XOR
0 0 0 1 0 0 0 0	16
1 1 0 0 0 1 1 1	199

As you can see our bit is now off, and the others haven't changed since the XOR leaves any other 1 unaltered.

Perfect. *But* – there's a problem. What if our bit was *already* off? This is what happens if we apply an XOR:

Binary	Decimal
1 1 0 0 0 1 1 1 XOR	199 XOR
0 0 0 1 0 0 0 0	16
1 1 0 1 0 1 1 1	215

The result is wrong! Our bit was off and has been turned *on*. Solution? We have to AND this result with the original value:

Binary	Decimal
1 1 0 0 0 1 1 1 XOR	199 XOR
0 0 0 1 0 0 0 0	16
1 1 0 1 0 1 1 1 AND	215 AND
1 1 0 0 0 1 1 1	199
1 1 0 0 0 1 1 1	199

If the bit was already off, it is turned on by the XOR, but the following AND turns it off again, leaving the other bits untouched, because each 1 is matched by another 1.

Does it impact the previous case, when the starting value was already 1? Let's check:

Binary	Decimal
1 1 0 1 0 1 1 1 XOR	215 XOR
0 0 0 1 0 0 0 0	16
1 1 0 0 0 1 1 1 AND	199 AND
1 1 0 1 0 1 1 1	215
1 1 0 0 0 1 1 1	199

We're lucky. The first XOR turns the bit off (as we saw previously), and the following AND doesn't change it, so the result is still correct.

I know this may sound a bit complicated if you hear it for the first time. Some time may be needed to digest every... *bit* of it (pun intended). But that's a good example of how the logical functions, apparently so simple, can be combined and exploited to build more complex structures and calculations.

In conclusion, this is the operation we need to perform to make sure that a single, specific bit is set to 0, whatever its starting value:

```
(V XOR mask) AND V
```

4. *Count the 1s*

    How can we count the number of students who attended a specific lesson? Of course, we have to count the 1s in the vector for that day.

    Now, there are several ways to perform this task. The most brutal is extracting all the bits one by one and count the 1s. But to do that, you first need to transform the decimal value into a string with its binary representation, and then you need a `For... Next` loop working on the string, extracting one character at a time with the `Mid()` function to check whether it's a 1. It works, but all of these steps are slow.

    There's a faster method, again based on binary arithmetic. Let's see what happens in the binary world when we subtract 1 from a number. We haven't seen how the subtraction works, but just focus on the result:

Binary	Decimal
1 0 0 1 0 1 0 0 -	148 -
1	1
1 0 0 1 0 0 1 1	147

See what happened? All the bits to the right of the rightmost 1 (here colored in green) have been flipped to their opposite, including the rightmost 1. Now, if we AND this result with the original value

Binary	Decimal
1 0 0 1 0 1 0 0 -	148 -
1	1
1 0 0 1 0 0 1 1 AND	147 AND
1 0 0 1 0 1 0 0	148
1 0 0 1 0 0 0 0	144

the net result is that we have turned off the rightmost 1 in the original number, leaving the other bits unchanged. Let's do another iteration using 144, the number we just got:

Binary	Decimal
1 0 0 1 0 0 0 0 -	144 ·
1	1
1 0 0 0 1 1 1 1 AND	143 AND
1 0 0 1 0 0 0 0	144
1 0 0 0 0 0 0 0	128

Again, the subtraction flipped to their opposite all the bits to the right of the rightmost 1 (included). The following AND gets rid of the rightmost 1 of the starting number. See the point? Two iterations, two 1s have been eliminated. A third iteration would eliminate the third and last 1, bringing the vector value to 0.

So, to count the 1s, we can use a loop that repeats these operations until we get 0. The number of iterations will be the number of 1s in our vector:

```
Do Until (V=0)
    V = (V - 1) And V
Loop
```

OK, now we have all the theory we need to manipulate our vectors. We just have to translate it into VBA.

So, let's write a class to manipulate our vector and name it clsVector. It just needs one variable, the vector itself. To be more generic, we'll use a long, that is a 32 bit long value:

CLSVECTOR

Option Explicit

Private Vector As Long

This means we can handle up to 32 entities. Students, ingredients in a recipe, players in a team, employees in a business unit, rooms in a hotel, you name it. Unfortunately, that's the limit: we can't use a variable with more bits. But 32 entities are a fair amount and, in most cases, more than enough. If needed, you can use more Longs, with some additional efforts when writing our code to switch from one to another.

Now, let's assign the bits. We define an enumeration of what we called masks:

CLSVECTOR

```
Option Explicit

Private Vector As Long

Public Enum enmVectorMasks
  vmMASK0 = &H1
  vmMASK1 = &H2
  vmMASK2 = &H4
  vmMASK3 = &H8
  vmMASK4 = &H10
  vmMASK5 = &H20
  vmMASK6 = &H40
  vmMASK7 = &H80
  vmMASK8 = &H100
  vmMASK9 = &H200
  vmMASK10 = &H400
  vmMASK11 = &H800
  vmMASK12 = &H1000
  vmMASK13 = &H2000
  vmMASK14 = &H4000
  vmMASK15 = &H8000
  vmMASK16 = &H10000
  vmMASK17 = &H20000
  vmMASK18 = &H40000
  vmMASK19 = &H80000
  vmMASK20 = &H100000
  vmMASK21 = &H200000
  vmMASK22 = &H400000
  vmMASK23 = &H800000
  vmMASK24 = &H1000000
```

```
vmMASK25  =  &H2000000
vmMASK26  =  &H4000000
vmMASK27  =  &H8000000
vmMASK28  =  &H10000000
vmMASK29  =  &H20000000
vmMASK30  =  &H40000000
vmMASK31  =  &H80000000
End  Enum
```

Don't be afraid of the huge numbers; we will never have to deal with them from now on. In this case, I prefer to use the hexadecimal notation, which is more compact and somehow more readable. Maybe it's not easy to see it, if you're not well acquainted with the Hex code, but every value here is a power of 2, so each one addresses a specific bit in our vector, and no combination of masks addresses the same bit.

For example, if we want to operate on bit 2 and bit 5 at the same time, we can add their masks, using something like

```
v = vmMASK2 Or vmMASK5
```

which is &H2 + &H20 = 4 + 32, so 36 in decimal. Its binary representation is 00100100: as you can see, this is a combined mask addressing bit 2 and bit 5. And since no other mask combination adds up to 36, there is no chance that the same two bits can be addressed in any other way. Given any number, there is never any ambiguity on which bits we're going to change.

One side note: you may ask, "Why are you using OR instead of a normal + sign? What's wrong with v = vmMASK2 + vmMASK5, which is more intuitive?" Good question. After all, the result is the same with both operators. But I prefer the OR for two reasons:

1. We're dealing with Boolean logic, and I think an OR
   is more appropriate than a + sign, which doesn't
   belong to the Boolean realm. You'd never use OR
   when adding two numbers, so why should you use +
   when ORing two numbers?

2. The OR guarantees the result is always correct, the
   plus sign doesn't. I'll explain this better. You can
   execute the following operations in your Immediate
   Windows, so you can better follow what I mean.

Suppose I have a vector V, starting from 0. I turn bit 3 on:

```
V = vmMASK3
```

Its value is now &H8 = 8 decimal = 8_{dec}
Now I also want to turn bit 5 on. Using the OR

```
V = V OR vmMASK5
```

and the current value is now &H8 + &H20 = 8 + 32 = 40_{dec}.

Now, let's say this assignment is run again: it might be a bug in the
code, or something going on inside a loop, or any other reason:

```
V = V OR vmMASK5
```

The result is still 40 because the OR executes bit-by-bit operation in
the binary domain. It doesn't matter how many times you execute this
operation, the result will always be 40. And that's what we want.

What happens if we execute the same operations using the plus sign in
place of the OR? V
starts again from 0. Then we have

```
V = vmMASK3
```

so now V = 8. Let's turn bit 5 on:

```
V = V + vmMASK5
```

and V is now 40, which is correct. But, if we now execute this assignment again

```
V = V + vmMASK5
```

the current value (try typing ? V in the Immediate Window) is no longer 40, but 72: it's wrong! And that's because the plus sign is a *decimal* operation, so every time the assignment is executed, we're actually adding the number 32 to the vector as a whole. It's no longer a bit-by-bit operation; it's a normal decimal addition, and the final number is not what we expect.

That's why when we are manipulating the binary representations of numbers, rather than their actual values, I suggest using OR instead of the plus sign and AND instead of the multiplication sign.

Back to our class. The vector is initialized when the class is instantiated:

CLSVECTOR

```
Private Sub Class_Initialize()
  Vector = 0
End Sub
```

Actually, this is not needed, as VBA would consider it as 0 anyway, but I like to make all the operations explicit. And after all, this is just a convention. In other cases, the starting value might be different from 0, so this line makes the code a bit more generic.

OK. So, how do we set a bit to 1? We saw how to do that a few moments ago:

```
CLSVECTOR

Public Sub maskAdd(mask As enmVectorMasks)
  Vector = Vector Or mask
End Sub
```

We also know how to check if a bit is 1:

```
CLSVECTOR

Public Function isOn(mask As enmVectorMasks) As Boolean
  isOn = ((Vector AND mask) > 0)
End Function
```

And we also know how to turn a bit off, regardless of its current value:

```
CLSVECTOR

Public Sub maskRemove(mask As enmVectorMasks)
  Vector = (Vector Xor mask) And Vector
End Sub
```

And remember how can we count the 1s in a vector? We just have to use locVector, a local copy of the global vector, as the function modifies its original value:

```
                        CLSVECTOR

Public Property Get count1s() As Integer
Dim retVal As Integer
Dim locVector As Long

  retVal = 0
  locVector = Vector

  Do Until (locVector = 0)
    locVector = (locVector - 1) And locVector
    retVal = retVal + 1
  Loop

  count1s = retVal
End Property
```

Again: if you prefer to use a different method, there are many to choose from. But this is extremely fast, as it uses binary and arithmetic operations only, no string and no VBA functions. And most of all, a number of iterations equals to the number of 1s in the vector, regardless of the actual number of bits. So, for example, counting the 1s in 100 and in 100000000000000000 takes exactly the same time: 1 iteration.

Of course, at some point, we may need to know the current value of the vector, but that's trivial:

```
                        CLSVECTOR

Public Property Get Value() As Long
  Value = Vector
End Property
```

And since we're here, we can also add a method to reset its value:

CLSVECTOR

```
Public Sub Reset(Optional startWith As Long = 0)
  Vector = startWith
End Sub
```

Finished. This is the class that handles a binary vector and implements the bit-field technique.

How do we use this class in our code? Well, just like any other class. We create an instance (again, you can execute these operations in the Immediate Window):

```
Set c = new clsVector
```

Then we can call its methods. For example, turn bit 7 on:

```
c.maskAdd vmMASK7
```

If you print the vector value (? c.Value in the Immediate Window), you get 128. Let's turn on another couple of bits:

```
c.MaskAdd vmMASK2 OR vmMASK9
```

and we end up with a value of 128 + 4 + 512 = 644, whose binary representation is 1010000100. As you can see, the only bits set to 1 are those we expected: bit 2, bit 7, and bit 9.

Now turn bit 7 off:

```
c.maskRemove vmMASK7
```

And the current value is now 644 – 128 = 516, 1000000100 in binary: bit 7 has been correctly turned off.

How many 1s are in this number?

```
? c.count1s
```

returns 2, which is correct: only bits 2 and 9 are currently on. You could play some more on your own, turning bits on and off and checking the results.

And that's it. This class can be imported into your applications as it is, and it's ready to be used. Create an instance, and you're set to go. Of course, you can rename the enumeration items to match your needs, for example, vmSALT, vmSUGAR, vmCOFFEE, vmFLOUR, and such, if you're handling ingredients; vmROOM1, vmROOM2, and vmROOM3, if you're dealing with a hotel; or vmSTUDENT1, vmSTUDENT2, and vmSTUDENT3, if you're running a class, whatever is more appropriate to your situation (I keep the vm prefix to match my personal preferences, but of course, you can choose whatever name matches *your* preferences).

Now, as promised, I'll show you a fast way to translate a binary number into its decimal equivalent. Suppose we have the number 110101, and we want to convert it to decimal. Here's how it works.

We start from the left and count 1:

1

1   1   0   1   0   1

Then we move to the right and double our number:

$1 \xrightarrow{\times 2} 2$

1   1   0   1   0   1

So now we have 2. We are over a 1, so add it:

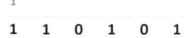

1   1   0   1   0   1

We get 3. Move again, and double:

$$3 \xrightarrow{\times 2} 6$$

1	1	0	1	0	1

We have now 6. We are over a 0, so disregard it. Or add it anyway; it doesn't change much. Our running total is still 6.

Move again, and double:

$$6 \xrightarrow{\times 2} 12$$

1	1	0	1	0	1

We've got 12, but we are over a 1, so add it:

$$6 \xrightarrow{\times 2} 13$$
↑ Add

1	1	0	1	0	1

And now we have 13. Move and double again:

$$13 \xrightarrow{\times 2} 26$$

1	1	0	1	0	1

The running total is 26, and since we're over a 0, it doesn't change. Move and double again:

$$26 \xrightarrow{\times 2} 52$$

1	1	0	1	0	1

and add the 1:

$$26 \xrightarrow{\times 2} 53$$
↑ Add

1	1	0	1	0	1

And we're there: $110101_{bin} = 53_{dec}$. It probably looks more difficult than it actually is, so let's do one more. But this time with no graphic, just follow the steps on the number itself, and you'll see how easy the whole process is.

- The number is **101011**.

- Start with 1.

- Move and double: we have 2, plus 0 is 2.

- Move and double: 4, plus 1 is 5.

- Move and double: 10, plus 0 is 10.

- Move and double: 20, plus 1 is 21.

- Move and double: 42, plus 1 is 43.

Done. Easy and fast.

3.1. Conclusion

OK, we're done with the bit-field thing. You'll probably want to read this part again and again to make sure you understand how it works. I can tell you the time you spend on it is going to be well spent, as this presence vector can be useful in many situations, even when its usefulness is not immediately evident. In our case, we'll use it to place objects on our scrolling timeline.

CHAPTER 4

Advanced Interfaces: Drag and Drop

...where we create something "different":

- A drag-and-drop engine
- The "ghost label" effect
- Sliding subforms

So far, we haven't seen anything really new, I know. I gave you my version of "good" practices, and we covered most of what's necessary to know about classes. These first two parts were needed, though, to lay the foundations on which we'll found this third part. Here, I will generously use all the concepts we have been talking about so far to build some innovative interfaces, what I like to call *dynamic* interfaces.

Why innovative? Well, as I said in the introduction, I don't know any other Access programmer who has ever produced anything similar, to the best of my knowledge. I'm not bragging, please trust me, I'm just stating a fact as a consequence of my participation at the DevCon 2021.

To start, I'll show you the technique at the base of (almost) every dynamic interface: how to drag an image. Then we'll connect two of these draggable images with lines, which remain "attached" to the corresponding images while they are dragged around, and then we'll add more images and more lines. At the end of this discussion, you'll have a class you can easily embed in any of your Access applications.

A variation of this class will be used to drag a label instead of an image, using what I call the "ghost label" effect.

Then, I'll show you how to use another variation of the dragging technique to create a "sliding forms" effect with subforms, and finally the most complex application of all, a scrolling timetable where objects can be dynamically placed.

The first things will be easier, but they'll quickly get rather complicated. Anyway, I'm not going to drop the code from above as revealed truth. Not only am I going to build it from scratch, but I will also try to explain every single line of code. I'm aware this approach may perhaps introduce too many details, which may lead to some confusion at first, but I believe it's necessary to reach a deep understanding of the whole engine and it will also be useful to understand how these kinds of interfaces were born and the kind of problems one can face during the process.

So, grab some liters of coffee, and let's start this long and hard journey.

4.1. How to Make an Image Draggable

Let's start from scratch, creating a new database. The first thing to do is go to `File.Options.Current` (shortcuts: Alt+F, T, C) and set `Overlapping Windows` on (shortcuts: Alt+O). We have to close and reopen the database, but compacting will do as well.

Now, create a form with `Create.Form Design` (Alt+C, FD). Then go to the `Format` tab in the Property Sheet and set the border style to `thin`, disable the record selectors and the navigation buttons, and get rid of the scrolling bars as well.

The only asset we need is an image. Any image will do, so go to `Form Design.Insert.Image.Browse...` and feel free to choose any image you prefer. Let's name it `imgDrag` to give it a meaningful name. We can now start writing our code. Switch to the code editor, create a class module, and save everything. The form can be saved with the default name, we don't care, and we can name the class `clsDrag`.

Let's start declaring some variables. Of course, I'm going to use a UDT (user-defined type). We need just a few variables. First of all, two `Single` variables to keep track of the image position. Then, since we want to confine the draggable image within the form boundaries, we also need to know the form dimensions. And finally, a `Boolean` variable to turn the dragging on and off:

CLSDRAG

```
Option Explicit

Private Type recLocals
    dX As Single          ' Left position of the mouse
                            '    (relative to the image left)
                            '    when the image is grabbed
    dY As Single          ' Top position of the mouse
                            '    (relative to the image top)
                            '    when the image is grabbed
    formW As Single       ' Width of the container form
    formH As Single       ' Height of the container form
    Dragging As Boolean   ' TRUE when the user grabs the image
End Type

Private Locals As recLocals
```

We also need one more variable of type Image, which will allow us to link the class instance to the image control on the screen. Since the image will be draggable, it will have to trigger some events, so we need it to appear in the list of objects with events (Figure 4-1).

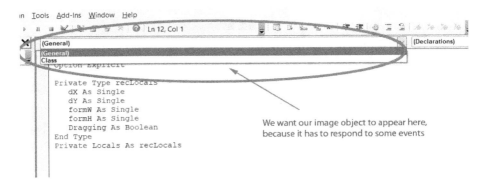

Figure 4-1. *Objects with events*

To make it appear there, we must declare it using the keyword WithEvents, but VBA doesn't allow such a WithEvents variable to be embedded within a UDT, so we have to declare it outside the structure:

```
                        CLSDRAG
```

```
Option Explicit

Private Type recLocals
    dX As Single            ' Left position of the mouse
                            '    (relative to the image left)
                            '    when the image is grabbed
    dY As Single            ' Top position of the mouse
                            '    (relative to the image top)
                            '    when the image is grabbed
    formW As Single         ' Width of the container form
    formH As Single         ' Height of the container form
    Dragging As Boolean     ' TRUE when the user grabs the image
```

```
End Type
Private Locals As recLocals
```

Private WithEvents myImage As Image

As you can see in Figure 4-2, now it's shown in the object list.

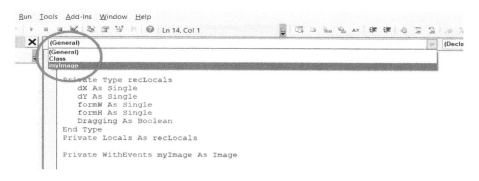

Figure 4-2. *Objects with events*

First things first, let's initialize the class. A class initialization is seldom needed in VBA, as you know that VBA sets a default value for a variable that's used for the first time, but I always prefer to make everything explicit, for I think it makes it easier to maintain the code and also to remember, after some time, what is what and what I wanted to do. So:

CLSDRAG

```
Option Explicit

[...]

Private Sub Class_Initialize()
    ' Basic variable initialization
    With Locals
        .Dragging = False
        .dX = 0
```

```
      .dY = 0
      .formH = 0
      .formW = 0
   End With
   Set myImage = Nothing
End Sub

Private Sub Class_Terminate()
      ' Clear memory
   Set myImage = Nothing
End Sub
```

As you can see, these are standard values, the same values that VBA would assume, but – again – I like to make this all explicit. What we should never forget, though, is to release the object memory when the class terminates. In this case, the only object we have is myImage, and we used the Terminate() event to assign it to Nothing.

We can now start writing our "real" code, and the first thing we need is an "init" function because the class needs to know which image has to be moved and the form dimensions, to limit its movements:

```
                        CLSDRAG

Public Sub Init(img As Image, formW As Single, formH As Single)
      ' Called by the form.
      ' Links the class to the image on it,
      ' and stores the form dimensions

   Set myImage = img
   Locals.formH = formH
   Locals.formW = formW

End Sub
```

We said that the image has to respond to some events for the drag to work. We are obviously talking about three events: mouseDown() (when the user presses the mouse button to grab the image), mouseMove() (when the mouse is moved, with the button still pressed, to move the image) and mouseUp() (to stop the movement and release the image).

These three events must be set up for our image. Now, we could leave this task to the user: in the Property Sheet for the image, the user has to click the Event tab and set [Event Procedure] for the three events. But we can't rely on the users to know and remember this fundamental step (or, if you prefer, we can graciously relieve them from this boring task...), so we'll do it via code:

```
                              CLSDRAG

Public Sub Init(img As Image, formW As Single, formH As Single)
  Set myImage = img
  Locals.formH = formH
  Locals.formW = formW

  myImage.OnMouseDown = "[Event Procedure]"
  myImage.OnMouseMove = "[Event Procedure]"
  myImage.OnMouseUp = "[Event Procedure]"

End Sub
```

Let's now write these three events. The first is myImage_mouseDown() – that's when the user clicks on the image to start dragging it. We have to do two things: the first is telling the rest of the class that the dragging has started, and this is the role of the variable we called Dragging:

```
CLSDRAG
```

Private Sub myImage_MouseDown(Button As Integer, Shift As
Integer, _ X As Single, Y As Single)
    ' The user "grabs" the image: start dragging

  With Locals
    .Dragging = True   ' Alert the rest of the code
                        '   that the dragging has started

  End With
End Sub

The second is storing the starting point, so that later we can calculate the movement amount, and that's what dX and dY are for:

```
CLSDRAG
```

```
Private Sub myImage_MouseDown(Button As Integer, Shift As
Integer, _ X As Single, Y As Single)
   With Locals
     .Dragging = True
     .dX = X              ' Store mouse left (relative to image)
     .dY = Y              ' Store mouse top (relative to image)
   End With

End Sub
```

Keep in mind that these values, X and Y, are relative to the image left and the image top, not to the screen or the form.

That's it for this event. We can write the mouseUp() straight away, as it is immediate, for all it has to do is telling the code that the dragging has stopped:

CLSDRAG

```
Private Sub myImage_MouseUp(Button As Integer, Shift As Integer,
_ X As Single, Y As Single)
    ' The user releases the mouse: stop dragging

    Locals.Dragging = False      ' Alert the rest of the code
                                 '    that the dragging has stopped

End Sub
```

The real magic is concentrated in the mouseMove(). The mouseMove() event is triggered when the user hovers the mouse over the image. In normal conditions, nothing has to happen. Only when the user has clicked the mouse and is keeping the mouse button down, the movement must be executed. But we know when this happens, as we have the variable called Dragging, which became True when the mouse button was pressed:

CLSDRAG

```
Private Sub myImage_MouseMove(Button As Integer, Shift As
Integer, _ X As Single, Y As Single)
    ' The user moves the mouse
```

```
With Locals
  If .Dragging Then

  End If
End With

End Sub
```

Then we have to calculate the new position for the image. The new left value *should be* the current position plus X minus dX:

```
                        CLSDRAG
```

```
Private Sub myImage_MouseMove(Button As Integer, Shift As
Integer, _ X As Single, Y As Single)
Dim newX As Single

  With Locals
    If .Dragging Then
          ' HORIZONTAL AXIS
      newX = myImage.Left + (X - .dX)     ' New image left?
    End If
  End With

End Sub
```

Why is that?

Consider this a "snapshot" of the moment the user presses the mouse button. dX is the position of the mouse, relative to the image left.

Now, the user (keeping the mouse button down) moves the mouse to the right. The X in the image is the current position of the mouse during the movement, passed as a parameter to the mouseMove().

Then, the difference X - .dX represents the number of pixels *the mouse* has been moved (horizontally) since the image was grabbed; that's to say, the number of pixels *the image* has to be moved (horizontally) if we want it to stay with the mouse. If the mouse has been moved to the right, as shown in this image, then it will be a positive quantity because X is greater than dX.

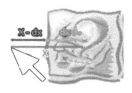

If, as shown in this fourth image, the mouse has been moved to the left, then X - .dX will be a negative quantity because X is less than dX.

In any case, X - .dX is an offset that, when added to the current image left position, gives the potential new left position of the image.

Before going on, let's define a constant named BORDER:

CLSDRAG

```
Private Sub myImage_MouseMove(Button As Integer, Shift As
Integer, _ X As Single, Y As Single)
Dim newX as Single

    Const BORDER = 10          ' Border around the image

    With Locals
      If .Dragging Then
        newX = myImage.Left + (X - .dX)

      End If
    End With

End Sub
```

We'll use this constant to leave a thin border all around the image, for aesthetic reasons: otherwise, the image might look "too close" to the form boundary, and this is not nice to see. In some cases, the peripheral pixels might even seem to "go out" of the screen. This doesn't happen if the image already has itself a border, but in general, it's better to enforce a small, 5–10 pixel border so that this effect is reduced for any image you may want to use.

How do we check if this new left position is good? We said the image must stay within the containing form. So, if newX is less than the border we want to maintain, then we're going way too left. If this happens, we have to stop the movement, so we force the new position to BORDER:

CLSDRAG

```
Private Sub myImage_MouseMove(Button As Integer, Shift As
Integer, _ X As Single, Y As Single)
Dim newX as Single

   Const BORDER = 10

   With Locals
     If .Dragging Then
       newX = myImage.Left + (X - .dX)
       If (newX < BORDER) Then
               ' Moving the image way too left
               ' Stop the movement to keep the image within
               the form
          newX = BORDER
       Else

       End If
     End If
   End With

End Sub
```

Let's now see what happens on the other side when the user moves the mouse to the right. Here, the situation is a bit more complicated. These images should help clarify the thing:

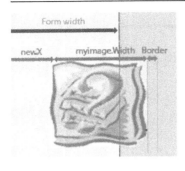

If newX (what should be the new image left position) plus the image width, plus the border we want to keep, is greater than the form width, then the right edge of the image is out of the container, and we have to block the movement before that happens. In what position exactly?

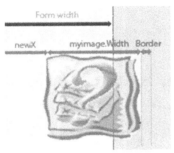

Well, it should be clear that the position we're looking for is the form width, minus the border, minus the image width.

Let's translate all of this into VBA:

CLSDRAG

```
Private Sub myImage_MouseMove(Button As Integer, Shift As
Integer, _ X As Single, Y As Single)
Dim newX as Single

  Const BORDER = 10

  With Locals
    If .Dragging Then
      newX = myImage.Left + (X - .dX)
      If (newX < BORDER) Then
        newX = BORDER
```

```
ElseIf (newX + myImage.Width + BORDER > .formW) Then
            ' Moving the image way too right
            ' Stop the movement to keep the image within
            the form
        newX = .formW - BORDER - myImage.Width
      End If
    End If
  End With

End Sub
```

On the vertical axis, the thing is totally similar, replacing Width with Height, Left with Top, and so on:

CLSDRAG

```
Private Sub myImage_MouseMove(Button As Integer, Shift As
Integer, _ X As Single, Y As Single)
Dim newX as Single, newY as Single

  Const BORDER = 10

  With Locals
    If .Dragging Then
      newX = myImage.Left + (X - .dX)
      If (newX < BORDER) Then
        newX = BORDER
      ElseIf (newX + myImage.Width + BORDER > .formW) Then
        newX = .formW - BORDER - myImage.Width
      End If

          ' VERTICAL AXIS
      newY = myImage.Top + (Y - .dY)
      If (newY < BORDER) Then
```

```
      newY = BORDER
    ElseIf (newY + myImage.Height + BORDER > .formH) Then
      newY = .formH - BORDER - myImage.Height
    End If
  End If
End With

End Sub
```

At this point, I'm guaranteed that newX and newY are two values that keep the image within the form, so I can assign them to the image itself:

```
                        CLSDRAG
```

```
Private Sub myImage_MouseMove(Button As Integer, Shift As
Integer, _ X As Single, Y As Single)
Dim newX As Single, newY As Single

  Const BORDER = 10

  With Locals
    If .Dragging Then
      newX = myImage.Left + (X - .dX)
      If (newX < BORDER) Then
        newX = BORDER
      ElseIf (newX + myImage.Width + BORDER > .formW) Then
        newX = .formW - BORDER - myImage.Width
      End If

      newY = myImage.Top + (Y - .dY)
      If (newY < BORDER) Then
        newY = BORDER
```

```
    ElseIf (newY + myImage.Height + BORDER > .formH) Then
        newY = .formH - BORDER - myImage.Height
    End If

        ' The image moves
    myImage.Move newX, newY
    End If
  End With

End Sub
```

In this very moment, the image moves on the screen following the mouse.

And the class is over. That's it, nothing else. As you can see, very short and rather simple, as it's all about calculating the image's new position. The rest of the code is trivial.

So, let's recap. When the users click on the image (with ANY button, since we don't check which button has actually been pressed), they "grab" the image, .Dragging becomes True, and the click position is stored in .dX and .dY. The following calls to mouseMove() are then processed (because .Dragging = True), and the image is moved – if possible. When the user releases the button, .Dragging is set to False, and the following mouseMove() calls have no effect.

Let's save and go back to our form. We must write some code for the form to activate the class, so in the form module, declare a variable, which we can call obj, and instantiate it in the Load() event. Then we can call our Init() function to pass the actual image control (whose name is imgDrag) and the form dimensions. And when the form closes, we have to free the memory allocated for our objects, in this case only obj:

```
┌─────────────────────────────────────────────────────────────┐
│                            FORM                               │
└─────────────────────────────────────────────────────────────┘

Option Explicit

Private obj As clsDrag

Private Sub Form_Load()
        ' Create and init a class instance
    Set obj = New clsDrag
    obj.Init imgDrag, Me.InsideWidth, Me.InsideHeight
End Sub

Private Sub Form_Close()
    ' Clear the memory
    Set obj = Nothing
End Sub
```

Done. The code is over; nothing else is needed. When the form is opened, the object is created and linked to the image. From now on, the class itself will handle all the events. As you can see, if you run the form, you can "bang" against the form edges, and you can't go any further because of the checks we implemented in the mouseMove()event. The picture always maintains a 10-pixel distance from any edge.

The form just creates and destroys the object, and the process is completely independent from the image and form sizes. In fact, if you change the image size and/or the form size, everything still works as expected, with no modifications to the code.

4.2. Adding More Images

How hard is it to add more images? Well, we have a class. It literally takes seconds.

Add a new image to the form (it doesn't have to be the same image, nor does it have to be the same size), and name it imgDrag2. To be consistent, also rename the first image as imgDrag1 and the first object in the form code as obj1. The class needs no modifications; just duplicate the form code:

```
                              FORM

Option Explicit

Private obj1 As clsDrag
Private obj2 As clsDrag

Private Sub Form_Load()
  ' Create and init a class instance (first image)
  Set obj1 = New clsDrag
  obj1.Init imgDrag1, Me.InsideWidth, Me.InsideHeight

  ' Create and init anot her class instance (second image)
  Set obj2 = New clsDrag
  obj2.Init imgDrag2, Me.InsideWidth, Me.InsideHeight
End Sub

Private Sub Form_Close()
  Set obj1 = Nothing
  Set obj2 = Nothing
End Sub
```

Save, run the form, and we now have two draggable images totally independent from each other.

Can we have more? Of course, we have a class! We could add a third, then a fourth, then a fifth image and clone the code again and again. Everything will work. The only problem is that when the images are more than three or four, the code starts to grow a bit too much: for each image, we need to create another variable and duplicate all the code. Not quite elegant, and inefficient for sure. So, how can we make things a bit more manageable? A possible solution is using an array.

Say, we want to use four images, as shown in Figure 4-3. Of course, they can be of any size, not necessarily the same.

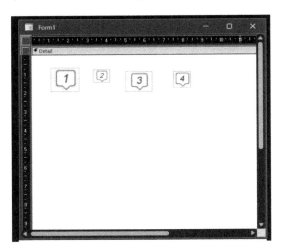

Figure 4-3. *List of procedures*

Name them imgDrag1, imgDrag2, imgDrag3, and imgDrag4. The important thing here is that the numbering is sequential, for this will simplify our code, as we will see in a moment.

Now, switch to the code editor, and in the form module, delete the existing code. Let's start again by creating a constant with the number of images to make things a bit more generic:

FORM

```
Option Explicit
Private Const MAX_IMAGES = 4
```

Now, basically we rewrite the same code we wrote before for two images but in a generalized form to handle a whole array of images:

```
                              FORM

Option Explicit

Private Const MAX_IMAGES = 4

Dim obj() As clsDrag

Private Sub Form_Load()
Dim i As Byte

  ReDim obj(MAX_IMAGES)

    ' Create a class instance for each image
    For i = 1 To MAX_IMAGES
      Set obj(i) = New clsDrag                          ' 1
      obj(i).Init Me.Controls("imgDrag" & i), Me.InsideWidth, _
                             Me.InsideHeight            ' 2
  Next

End Sub

Private Sub Form_Close()
Dim i As Byte

  For i = 1 To MAX_IMAGES
    Set obj(i) = Nothing
  Next

End Sub
```

If you compare this code with the previous one, you'll see that it basically does the same exact operations. This time, though, we create an instance of the class for each image in the array (line *1*). You may also have noticed how the sequential numbering in the image names comes in handy, as we can initialize all the images using a single loop (code on line *2*).

And we're done. Just run the form, and you have four draggable objects completely independent from one another. Four, five, ten, at this point it's not important, because all we have to do now is just change the constant and add the images to the form, properly named, and the whole code will keep on working without any other change.

4.3. Connecting Two Images with Lines

Now, what can the next step be? Well, why not use lines to connect the images, as depicted in Figure 4-4? That would be a useful way to visually show relations between objects, for example.

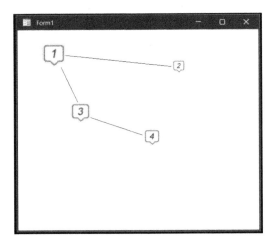

Figure 4-4. *Connecting images*

For now, we'll only use two images, so we delete imgDrag3 and imgDrag4 and only leave imgDrag1 and imgDrag2. Of course, we'll also need a line control, which we can name, for example, linLink. In the code, we'll just need to change the constant MAX_IMAGES, setting its value to 2, and everything should be working as before, of course without the line. If you run the form again, the two images are still independently draggable.

Back to our code. Our problem here is to place the line correctly, meaning that when an image moves, the line must move as well to follow its center. Now, it seems intuitive to write this code within the class itself, at the very moment when the image moves, that's to say the line highlighted here:

CLSDRAG

```
Private Sub myImage_MouseMove(Button As Integer, Shift As
Integer, _ X As Single, Y As Single)
          [...]
       myImage.Move newX, newY
          [...]
End Sub
```

Why don't we place here the code to move the line too and keep it connected to the image? In fact, it's not so simple. An instance of this class handles one single image and doesn't "know" about the line and doesn't even "know" that a second instance has been created. This is true in general, when we talk about classes: an instance of a class is an isolated object, which usually doesn't "know" whether other instances of its class, or of another class, exist – and most of all, doesn't have to! It's true that this information CAN be passed to the class (with a function, with one or more properties, or in any other way), but that would be a very dirty solution, somehow defeating the concept of object-oriented programming.

If not the class, it must be the form. The form "sees" everything: all the class instances and the line as well. Therefore, the form is the more logical place to insert this code.

So, let's create a sub named, say, Connect() in the form module.

```
                              FORM

Private Sub Connect()

End Sub
```

Now, to connect the images, the line should link the two image centers, so we need to know their coordinates. This is a piece of information that each class instance can provide because it belongs to the image they handle. We can imagine writing a class function or a property, say, Center(), and invoke it from the form:

```
                              FORM

Private Sub Connect()
   P1 = obj(1).Center()
   P2 = obj(2).Center()
End Sub
```

The problem is that the image center is a point, that's to say a couple of values x and y, not a single value, which is what a function – or a property – normally returns. As a possible solution, we could split this Center()

function/property in two functions/properties, say, X() and Y(), each returning one value as usual, and create four variables, like X1, Y1, X2, and Y2, something like:

```
                              FORM

Private Sub Connect()
  X1 = obj(1).X()
  Y1 = obj(1).Y()
  X2 = obj(2).X()
  Y2 = obj(2).Y()
End Sub
```

Some developers prefer to create another class with only two properties, X() and Y(), and use this class as returning value for the function we called Center(). But I don't like this solution at all: adding a whole class module just to handle two values is like shooting a fly with a gun. We can do something else, which I think is more elegant: let's create a module with a public structure, which we name recPoint, with two values X and Y:

```
                            MDLDRAG

Option Explicit

Public Type recPoint
    X As Single
    Y As Single
End Type
```

Why can't we create this structure in the class module, even though it sounds more obvious, as it's a type that is strictly related to the class? We already know why: VBA doesn't allow us to create public structures within a class. Private structures, yes – in fact, we already have one, recLocals – but no public ones. We need again to use this "companion" module, and to highlight this dependency, we name the module after the class: mdlDrag, so we know that the two go together.

That said, let's forget those cumbersome four lines in Connect() and restore the calls to Center() by P1 and P2, whose type is now obviously recPoint:

```
                              FORM

Private Sub Connect()
Dim P1 As recPoint, P2 As recPoint

    ' Ask the objects for their centers
  P1 = obj(1).Center()
  P2 = obj(2).Center()

End Sub
```

Now, we can write Center() in clsDrag. Rather than a function, I would use a property here, even though this is one of those cases when there's not a big difference. But considering this value as a *property* of the object sounds more logical to me:

```
                            CLSDRAG

Public Property Get Center() As recPoint
    ' Returns the center of "my" image

  Center.X = myImage.Left + myImage.Width / 2
  Center.Y = myImage.Top + myImage.Height / 2

End Property
```

Useless to say (but I'll say it anyway), this property returns the center of the image bounding box, not of the object depicted in the image itself. As long as the picture is symmetric with respect to the bounding box center, there is no difference. But keep this in mind, as this distinction might have some impact on the look and feel of your interface when you drag the images.

Back to the form, we now have these P1 and P2, which we can use to place the line. "Placing a line" means we have to define the following properties for the line we called linLink:

```
                            FORM

Private Sub Connect()
Dim P1 As recPoint, P2 As recPoint

  P1 = obj(1).Center()
  P2 = obj(2).Center()

  ' Resize and position the line to connect the images
  With linLink
    .Left =
    .Top =
    .Width =
    .Height =
    .LineSlant =
  End With

End Sub
```

Let's start with the .Left value. It should be clear that it is determined by the left position of the leftmost image, whichever it is, as shown in Figures 4-5 and 4-6.

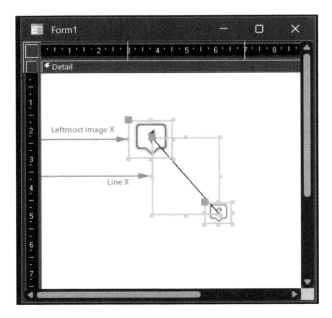

Figure 4-5. *Finding line .left (img1 above)*

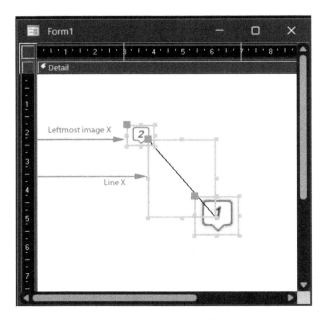

Figure 4-6. *Finding line .left (img2 above)*

```
                              FORM

Private Sub Connect()
Dim P1 As recPoint, P2 As recPoint

    P1 = obj(1).Center()
    P2 = obj(2).Center()

    With linLink
      .Left = IIf(P1.X < P2.X, P1.X, P2.X)
      .Top =
      .Width =
      .Height =
      .LineSlant =
    End With

End Sub
```

We can determine the .Top value of the line in a similar way, as it is given by the top coordinate of the topmost image, as shown in Figures 4-7 and 4-8.

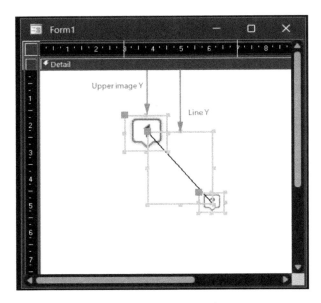

Figure 4-7. *Finding line .Top (img1 above)*

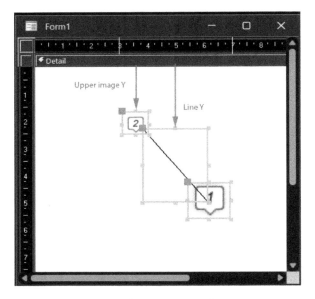

Figure 4-8. *Finding line .Top (img2 above)*

```
                              FORM

Private Sub Connect()
Dim P1 As recPoint, P2 As recPoint

    P1 = obj(1).Center()
    P2 = obj(2).Center()

    With linLink
      .Left = IIf(P1.X < P2.X, P1.X, P2.X)
      .Top = IIf(P1.Y < P2.Y, P1.Y, P2.Y)
      .Width =
      .Height =
      .LineSlant =
    End With

End Sub
```

.Width and .Height are also easy to find, as they are only determined by the distance between the two centers, regardless of the relative positions of the two images (Figures 4-9 to 4-12).

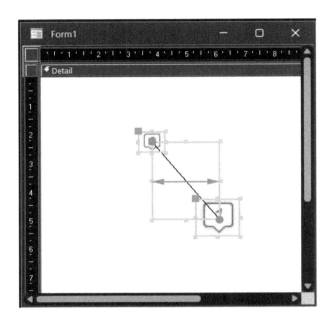

Figure 4-9. *Finding line .Width (img1 above)*

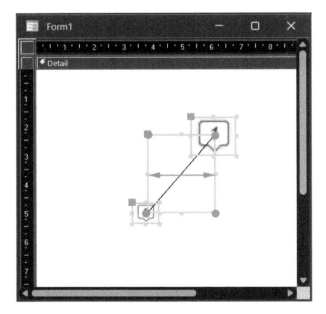

Figure 4-10. *Finding line .Width (img2 above)*

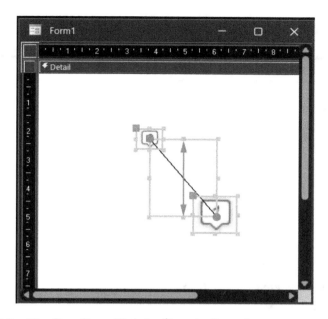

Figure 4-11. *Finding line .Height (img1 above)*

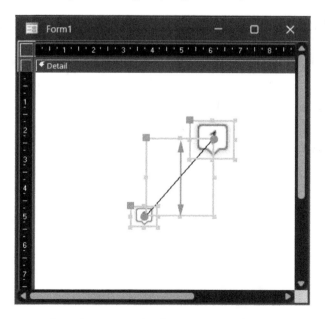

Figure 4-12. *Finding line .Height (img2 above)*

What matters is the absolute value of the distance, so we can write:

```
                              FORM
```

```
Private Sub Connect()
Dim P1 As recPoint, P2 As recPoint

  P1 = obj(1).Center()
  P2 = obj(2).Center()

  With linLink
    .Left = IIf(P1.X < P2.X, P1.X, P2.X)
    .Top = IIf(P1.Y < P2.Y, P1.Y, P2.Y)
    .Width = Abs(P1.X - P2.X)
    .Height = Abs(P1.Y - P2.Y)
    .LineSlant =
  End With

End Sub
```

Determining the value of .LineSlant is a bit trickier. Let's recall how it works: it's False when the line is a backslash (\); it's True when the line is a slash (/). Let's consider this latter case. The line should be a slash when either of the images, we don't know which, is *below* and *to the left* of the other one, as shown in Figures 4-13 and 4-14.

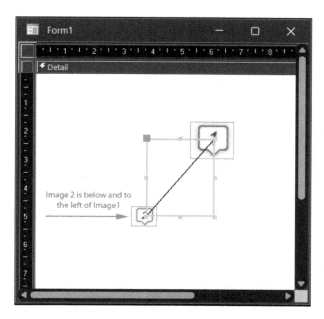

Figure 4-13. *Finding line .LineSlant (img1 above)*

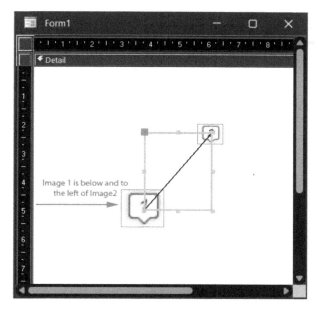

Figure 4-14. *Finding line .LineSlant (img2 above)*

We can describe this situation like this:

```
                              FORM

Private Sub Connect()
Dim P1 As recPoint, P2 As recPoint

  P1 = obj(1).Center()
  P2 = obj(2).Center()

  With linLink
    .Left = IIf(P1.X < P2.X, P1.X, P2.X)
    .Top = IIf(P1.Y < P2.Y, P1.Y, P2.Y)
    .Width = Abs(P1.X - P2.X)
    .Height = Abs(P1.Y - P2.Y)
    .LineSlant = ((P1.X < P2.X) And (P1.Y > P2.Y)) _
              Or ((P1.X > P2.X) And (P1.Y < P2.Y))
  End With

End Sub
```

- (P1.X < P2.X) And (P1.Y > P2.Y) means that image 1 is to the *left* of and *below* image 2.

- (P1.X > P2.X) And (P1.Y < P2.Y) means that image 1 is to the *right* of and *above* image 2.

In both cases, one image is below and to the left of the other one, so the Or between the two expressions returns True. If any of the conditions fail, then we have a different configuration, and .lineSlant gets the value False, making it a backslash.

We can call this function at the very start, in the Form_Load():

FORM

```
Private Sub Form_Load()
   [...]
   Connect
End Sub
```

So, as soon as the form is launched, the line is correctly placed. Try running the form several times, starting with different positions for the two images.

There are still two things to define. First, we see that the line is drawn "on" the images, and this is not nice to see. It's obviously a Z-order matter, so we just have to send the line to the background (right-click on the line, then Position.Send to back). Now, the line is under the images, and the visual effect is much nicer.

Second: we still need to move the line, for if we move either image, the line must follow. To solve this problem, we need to know *when* an image is moved, and obviously, the mouseMove() in the class module is the only spot in the code where this happens. The class, or better the instance, must tell the form that a movement has occurred so that the form can call Connect(), because at this moment in time, the form is totally unaware of whatever the images are doing. Remember that the form creates the instances and then delegates any action to the class. But this definitely complicates our lives because the best way to do this is to define an event, for example, Moved:

CLSDRAG

```
Option Explicit

Public Event Moved()

[...]
```

When the movement occurs, the instance raises the event:

```
                          CLSDRAG

Private Sub myImage_MouseMove(Button As Integer, Shift As
Integer, _ X As Single, Y As Single)
      [...]
      myImage.Move newX, newY
      RaiseEvent Moved
      [...]
End Sub
```

And this is a huge complication because the two objects now become "with events." But we *can't do that* because Access doesn't allow arrays of objects with events. If we try to define the array WithEvents, we immediately have an error:

```
                           FORM

Option Explicit

Private Const MAX_IMAGES = 4

Dim WithEvents obj() As clsDrag

 [...]
```

The brutal way to solve this problem is to go back to the previous version of the code, the one we saw earlier, so to have two separate objects, not an array. Of course, we don't need the constant anymore, and Connect() has to be modified too. Delete all the code in the form and replace it with the following:

FORM

```
Option Explicit

 ' Private Const MAX_IMAGES = 2

Private WithEvents obj1 As clsDrag
Private WithEvents obj2 As clsDrag

Private Sub Form_Load()
  Set obj1 = New clsDrag
  obj1.Init imgDrag1, Me.InsideWidth, Me.InsideHeight

  Set obj2 = New clsDrag
  obj2.Init imgDrag2, Me.InsideWidth, Me.InsideHeight

  Connect
End Sub

Private Sub Form_Close()
  Set obj1 = Nothing
  Set obj2 = Nothing
End Sub

Private Sub Connect()
Dim P1 As recPoint, P2 As recPoint

  P1 = obj1.Center()
  P2 = obj2.Center()

  With linLink
    .Left = IIf(P1.X < P2.X, P1.X, P2.X)
    .Top = IIf(P1.Y < P2.Y, P1.Y, P2.Y)
    .Width = Abs(P1.X - P2.X)
```

```
    .Height = Abs(P1.Y - P2.Y)
    .LineSlant = ((P1.X < P2.X) And (P1.Y > P2.Y)) _
              Or ((P1.X > P2.X) And (P1.Y < P2.Y))
End With

End Sub
```

What we have done is just re-expanding the two-element array back in two distinct variables, nothing else, so everything should still be working (try running the form again, and the line should still be correctly placed). What's still missing now is handling the event generated by the mouseMove(). Since we declared the objects WithEvents, we have access to their events – in this case, only one, Moved. The only thing to do here is to call Connect().

```
                              FORM

Private Sub obj1_Moved()
        ' Called by obj1 when it's moved
        ' Reposition the line
    Connect
End Sub

Private Sub obj2_Moved()
        ' Called by obj2 when it's moved
        ' Reposition the line
    Connect
End Sub
```

Let's recap: when the form loads, it creates two instances of our class, passing the two images to be moved. From now on, the class will handle all the relevant events (mouseDown(), mouseMove(),mouseUp()). When the user drags an image, the mouseMove() raises the event Moved, which is received by the container form, which asks the two images for their current positions and moves the line accordingly. As you can see, if you run the form now, the line slant is always correct, regardless of the relative position of the two objects. The drag rules are still valid, so the images are still blocked by the form edges, with a 10-pixel border.

4.4. Connecting Multiple Images

OK, this works for two images, but what happens if we need more? What if we want to connect more images? It's not so simple. This time, cloning the code wouldn't help because Connect() is built to handle two images only. Can you think of an easy way to modify it to handle, say, ten images? Not easy. In fact, we're going to see that this new requirement is going to have a devastating impact on our code. We'll have to change not only the code but the whole structure of our application.

Spoiler alert: This is NOT going to be as easy as the previous stuff!

There are probably several different solutions out there, but I think the one we're going to see is the best. At the cost of some complications in the code and the data structures, once completed, it is an extremely simple-to-use tool to handle any number of images, and it's a great chance to get acquainted with a very useful technique I use rather often in my projects. I call it "master-slave classes."

Disclaimer: This is not an invention of mine, but to be honest, I can't tell when or where I gave it a final shape and started using it. I probably derived it from hints and ideas found on the Web. I'm sorry if there's a legitimate owner out there I should mention and give credit to, but I sincerely have no idea.

It involves the use of two classes. Let's rename our clsDrag to clsSlave (of course, also rename mdlDrag to mdlSlave to keep consistency) and create a brand-new class, clsMaster:

```
                          CLSMASTER
```

Option Explicit

Since our problem is handling an array of objects with events, clsMaster is our solution. The user will create and interact with a *single* instance of this object, rather than an array of objects like before, so it can even be declared WithEvents if necessary. The Master will act as an intermediate layer between the form and the objects, doing the "dirty job," so to say, handling the array of images on behalf of the user, and communicating to the user (which means the form) the occurring events. Every image will be passed to clsSlave (formerly clsDrag), which will make it draggable and handle the drag events, exactly like before. This may sound confusing, but I hope it will become clearer as we proceed.

So, let's add again our four images (Figure 4-15) and rename them properly as imgDrag1, imgDrag2, imgDrag3, and imgDrag4. This time the numeration is important, as each number will work as an alias for the corresponding image. So, to the user, imgDrag1 will be "image 1," imgDrag2 will be "image 2," and so on.

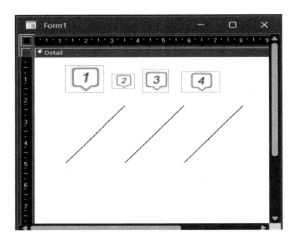

Figure 4-15. *Linking multiple images (design)*

Of course, we'll need some lines to connect our images. How many? Well, it depends on how many links we think we'll need. In this example, I will only make three links, so I'll use three lines. Of course, they can be more, but you'll have to estimate the correct amount.

Worst-case scenario, if you want each image to be connected to all the others, you will need $\dfrac{n(n-1)}{2}$ lines, being n the number of images. For example, if you have ten images and you want to connect each of them to all the others, you'll need $\dfrac{10(10-1)}{2} = 45$ lines.

The lines don't have to be named at all; the only thing we need to do is to send them to the background and make them invisible.

Let's switch to the form code. We will have to rewrite it completely, so we don't need most of the existing. What we'll still need is the constant MAX_IMAGES (of course, its value should be 4 now) and Connect(), so we keep them there for the moment. The rest of the code can be deleted.

```
                              FORM

Option Explicit

Private Const MAX_IMAGES = 4

    'Private Sub Connect()
    'Dim P1 As recPoint, P2 As recPoint
    '
    ' P1 = obj1.Center()
    ' P2 = obj2.Center()
    '
    ' With linLink
    '    .Left = IIf(P1.X < P2.X, P1.X, P2.X)
    '    .Top = IIf(P1.Y < P2.Y, P1.Y, P2.Y)
    '    .Width = Abs(P1.X - P2.X)
```

```
'    .Height = Abs(P1.Y - P2.Y)
'    .LineSlant = ((P1.X < P2.X) And (P1.Y > P2.Y)) _
'                 Or ((P1.X > P2.X) And (P1.Y < P2.Y))
' End With
'
'End Sub
```

Let's use a top-down approach. From a methodological point of view, I think the top-down approach is a particularly good one when you are designing a new system, as it's easier to see the things through the eyes of a user. And if we can put ourselves in our users' shoes, it will be easier to produce an effective and efficient interface. At least, that's what I usually do: I design the interface first and then find a way to implement it, no matter how complex it seems.

So, as we said, from the user's point of view, only one object must exist. Let's name it Master, of type clsMaster. We can instantiate it in the Form_Load() event and destroy it when the form is closed:

```
                              FORM

Option Explicit

Private Const MAX_IMAGES = 4

Private Master As clsMaster

Private Sub Form_Load()
  Set Master = New clsMaster
End Sub

Private Sub Form_Unload(Cancel As Integer)
  Set Master = Nothing
End Sub
```

In this example, our `clsMaster` will not trigger any event, but in case you need it, it will be possible to use `WithEvents`, as the code sees this variable as a single object, not an array. Now, if you think about it, since `Master` is an intermediary between the form and `clsSlave`, and `clsSlave` needs the form dimensions, `Master` has to pass this information to `clsSlave`. This means that the form has to pass this information to `Master`. We can imagine writing a function in the class to initialize everything that needs to be initialized:

```
                          FORM

Private Sub Form_Load()
      ' Create the Master instance and init it
   Set Master = New clsMaster
   Master.Init Me
End Sub
```

After that, for sure we need to pass the images to the class – in this case, only four, but can be any number. Again, we can imagine writing a function, say, `Add()`, to which we pass the images:

```
                          FORM

Private Sub Form_Load()
Dim i As Integer

   Set Master = New clsMaster
   Master.Init Me

      ' Pass the images to the Master
   For i = 1 To MAX_IMAGES
     Master.Add Me.Controls("imgDrag" & i)
   Next

End Sub
```

This loop works, again, because we named the images using progressive numbers.

Then we need another function, say, createLink(), to connect the images we want to connect. What I want to give the users is a simple syntax, for example:

FORM

```
Private Sub Form_Load()
Dim i As Integer

  Set Master = New clsMaster
  Master.Init Me

  For i = 1 To MAX_IMAGES
    Master.Add Me.Controls("imgDrag" & i)
  Next

  Master.createLink 1, 2        ' Link image1 to image2
  Master.createLink 1, 3        ' Link image1 to image3
  Master.createLink 2, 4        ' Link image2 to image4

End Sub
```

As we said, since I only have three lines, I can create three links only. And the images are stored in an array, so the numbers here represent their positions within the array. Of course, the users know nothing about the array, but each of these numbers (contained in the image names) appears to them as an intuitive alias for each image.

From the form point of view, the *user's* point of view, this is what we want to happen, and there's nothing else to add. We don't want to force the user to do any other operation. A simple and rather logical interface with our classes: creation, initialization, and links.

Following our top-down approach, let's create these methods in the class, so we'll remember to write them but postpone their exact definition:

```
                    CLSMASTER

Option Explicit

Public Sub Init(frm As Form)

End Sub

Public Sub Add(img As Image)

End Sub

Public Sub createLink(src As Integer, tgt As Integer)

End Sub
```

Before working on clsMaster, let's take a look at clsSlave. Previously, this class was handling the dragging of an image. It is still valid, as we still have to drag images. However, we obviously need to make some modifications. As before, every instance of this class will handle one single image on the form, but we said that all these images will be part of an array. With this master-slave technique, it's always useful to inform the slave in which array slot its object is placed. We'll use a variable named ndx to store this information.

The slave also needs to inform its Master when the image is moved. We can't use the event Moved, for (as we said) it's not possible to use events if the object is stored in an array: we have to find another method. The method we'll use needs another variable, say, Caller:

```
┌─────────────────────────────────────────────────────┐
│                     CLSSLAVE                          │
└─────────────────────────────────────────────────────┘

Private Type recLocals
  dX As Single
  dY As Single
  formW As Single
  formH As Single
  Dragging As Boolean
  ndx As Integer                ' Image position in the array
  Caller As clsMaster           ' Pointer to the Master class
End Type
Private Locals As recLocals
```

We can use the Init() function to add and initialize these new
variables (and remember to delete the object when the class terminates):

```
┌─────────────────────────────────────────────────────┐
│                     CLSSLAVE                          │
└─────────────────────────────────────────────────────┘

Private Sub Class_Terminate()
  Set myImage = Nothing
  Set Locals.Caller = Nothing
End Sub

Public Sub Init(ndx As Integer, img As Image, _
                        formW As Single, formH As Single, _
                Caller As clsMaster)
  Set myImage = img
  Locals.formH = formH
  Locals.formW = formW

  myImage.OnMouseDown = "[Event Procedure]"
  myImage.OnMouseMove = "[Event Procedure]"
  myImage.OnMouseUp = "[Event Procedure]"
```

```
Locals.ndx = ndx
Set Locals.Caller = Caller
End Sub
```

This `Caller` variable has a key role: it's an object pointing to the instance of `clsMaster`, and with that, we'll be able to call any public method in that instance.

The rest of the class remains more or less the same. `mouseDown()`, `mouseUp()`, and `Center()` don't change, while `mouseMove()` can't use the event, so we can delete the `RaiseEvent` line and its declaration:

CLSSLAVE

```
Option Explicit

Public Event Moved()              ' Delete this line

[...]

Private Sub myImage_MouseMove(Button As Integer, Shift As
Integer, _ X As Single, Y As Single)
        [...]
        myImage.Move newX, newY
        RaiseEvent Moved              ' Delete this line
        [...]
End Sub
```

But we need something here to replace it, something that raises an alert saying the image has been moved. Here is where we can use the variable `Caller`: rather than generating an event with `raiseEvent`, we can call a function in the parent class, a function we can still name `Moved()`.

```
                         CLSSLAVE

Private Sub myImage_MouseMove(Button As Integer, Shift As
Integer, _ X As Single, Y As Single)
        [...]
        myImage.Move newX, newY
        .Caller.Moved .ndx
        [...]
End Sub
```

and we'll pass the index of *this* image, so the caller knows who's being moved. This is the way we can simulate the raiseEvent mechanism and pass to the higher level class the relevant events (in this case, only mouseMove()). Basically, we're telling clsMaster "Hey Master, I'm the image number ndx, and I am being moved."

clsSlave is done; there's nothing else to add. It's time to tackle clsMaster.

First, create this new function Moved(), which as we just saw gets an integer as a parameter:

```
                         CLSMASTER

Public Sub Moved(ndx As Integer)

End Sub
```

Now, let's complete the Init() function. Define a variable to hold the calling form, and release it when the class terminates:

CLSMASTER

```
Option Explicit

Private Caller As Form

Public Sub Init(frm As Form)
  Set Caller = frm
End Sub

Private Sub Class_Terminate()
  Set Caller = Nothing
End Sub
```

As we said, this class will handle an array of draggable images, something like

```
Private Slaves() As ...
```

Now, instinctively, we might say that this array's type is `clsSlave`. But it's NOT going to be that simple. An image here, a so-called "slave," is a more complex object than just an image control on the form, because along with the image, we must also store its outgoing links, which connect it to other images. We can say that its links are somehow "part" of the image. And a structure is, again, the best way to collect related pieces of information. Let's then define another UDT:

CLSMASTER

```
Option Explicit

Private Caller As Form

' Type of "slave" objects
Private Type recSlave
```

```
    Slave As clsSlave                    ' The (draggable) image
    Edges() As ...                       ' List of outgoing links
End Type
Private Slaves() As recSlave             ' The array of
                                           "slave" objects
```

This structure embeds the usual clsSlave object (that's to say the draggable image, responding to the usual events) plus an array of lines. Since these lines won't have to trigger any event, an array is a reasonable way to store them.

But what type should this array be? The standard VBA Line? Let's think about what a *link* is. Again, a link is not only the line itself, the physical control on the form: we also need to know which image it connects. So, we need two pieces of information for each line. It seems logical to create another structure to model a "link" (I'll rather call it *edge* for historical and personal reasons):

CLSMASTER

```
Option Explicit

Private Caller As Form

    ' Type of a "link"
Private Type recEdge
    ctl As Line                          ' The physical line on the form
    targetImageNdx As Integer            ' Index of the linked image
End Type
```

recEdge.ctl is the physical line control on the form, while recEdge.targetImageNdx is the array index of the target image, that's to say the image connected by this edge.

Of course, now the type of our edge array is recEdge:

CLSMASTER

```
Option Explicit

Private Type recEdge
  ctl As Line
  targetImageNdx As Integer
End Type

Private Type recSlave
  Slave As clsSlave
  Edges() As recEdge
End Type
Private Slaves() As recSlave
```

So, every item in the array Slaves() has a draggable image (Slave) and a set of links (Edges()), where every link is a line (ctl) landing on another image (targetImageNdx).

If this point is clear, the next steps should be rather simple.

We have to initialize the arrays and destroy all objects when the instance terminates:

CLSMASTER

```
Public Sub Init(frm As Form)
  Set Caller = frm
  ReDim Slaves(0)
End Sub

Private Sub Class_Terminate()
Dim s As Integer, l As Integer
```

```
Set Caller = Nothing

For s = 1 To UBound(Slaves)
  With Slaves(s)
    Set .Slave = Nothing
    For l = 1 To UBound(.Edges)
        Set .Edges(l).ctl = Nothing
    Next
  End With
Next

End Sub
```

Let's now write Add( ), which gets an image and adds it to the array. The code is rather straightforward:

```
                            CLSMASTER
```

```
Public Sub Add(img As Image)
' Receives an image from the form and add it to the array
Dim ndx As Integer

    ndx = UBound(Slaves) + 1
    ReDim Preserve Slaves(ndx)
    With Slaves(ndx)                                      ' 1
      Set .Slave = New clsSlave                           ' 2
      .Slave.Init ndx, img, _
            Caller.InsideWidth, Caller.InsideHeight, Me   ' 3
      ReDim .Edges(0)                                     ' 4
    End With

End Sub
```

It creates a new slot in the array (line 1), in which a slave object is created (line 2). This slave is then initialized (line 3) passing its position in the array, the physical image control on the form, the form dimensions, and a reference (Me) to *this* class. Here's the trick to replace the raiseEvent method. We provide each slave with a pointer to this class, so it will be able to communicate with it. The Edge() array is also initialized (line 4).

So, let's recap. The form creates a *single* object, with or without events (in our case without), of type clsMaster, binds it to the relevant images, and tells it to create the needed links. And this is what the user sees.

clsMaster receives these images, adds them to an array, and makes them draggable by passing them to clsSlave which handles the dragging. The trick is to pass to every slave a pointer to clsMaster so that they will be able to call its method Moved().

We still need createLink() to connect two objects, source and target.

First, we need a line: following our top-down approach, let's say we have a "magic function" that will provide us with an available line and postpone its definition.

CLSMASTER

```
Public Sub createLink(src As Integer, tgt As Integer)
Dim lin As Line

  ' Get an available line on the form
  Set lin = getFreeLine()

End Sub

Private Function getFreeLine() As Line

End Function
```

We then place this line *somehow*, connecting source and target, using another function:

```
                            CLSMASTER

Public Sub createLink(src As Integer, tgt As Integer)
Dim lin As Line

  Set lin = getFreeLine()

  ' Use the line to connect image <src> to image <tgt>
  placeLink src, tgt, lin

End Sub

Private Sub placeLink(src As Integer, tgt As Integer, lin
As Line)

End Sub
```

Now, since we're adding a new edge connecting src and tgt, we have to update both slaves' arrays to include it. Let's first update the source image:

```
                            CLSMASTER

Public Sub createLink(src As Integer, tgt As Integer)
Dim lin As Line, ndx As Integer

  Set lin = getFreeLine()
  placeLink src, tgt, lin

  ' Create the "logical" link from image <src>'s point of view
  With Slaves(src)
```

```
    ndx = UBound(.Edges) + 1              ' 1
    ReDim Preserve .Edges(ndx)

    With .Edges(ndx)
      Set .ctl = lin                      ' 2
      .targetImageNdx = tgt               ' 3
    End With
  End With

End Sub
```

We first add a new slot to the array (line 1), to which we assign the line control on the form (line 2) and the index of the linked image (line 3).

But if this line goes from src to tgt, it also goes from tgt to src, so we must update the target image instance as well. The code is almost the same: just replace src with tgt. At the end, we release the memory:

```
                        CLSMASTER

Public Sub createLink(src As Integer, tgt As Integer)
Dim lin As Line, ndx As Integer

  Set lin = getFreeLine()
  placeLink src, tgt, lin

  With Slaves(src)
    ndx = UBound(.Edges) + 1
    ReDim Preserve .Edges(ndx)

    With .Edges(ndx)
      Set .ctl = lin
      .targetImageNdx = tgt
    End With
  End With
```

```
      ' Create the "logical" link from image <tgt>'s
      point of view
  With Slaves(tgt)
    ndx = UBound(.Edges) + 1
    ReDim Preserve .Edges(ndx)

    With .Edges(ndx)
      Set .ctl = lin
      .targetImageNdx = src
    End With
  End With

    ' Clear the memory
    Set lin = Nothing
End Sub
```

Let's now write the getFreeLine(), which is quite simple. We just
need to recall that at design time, we set all the lines to invisible. So, to find
the next available line, we can just iterate on all the controls on the form
(Caller) looking for an invisible line. When it's found, we set it to visible
(so the next call of getFreeLine() will disregard it), and we return it.

```
                        CLSMASTER
```

```
Private Function getFreeLine() As Line
  ' Finds and returns an available line on the form
  Dim retVal As Line, ctl As Control

    For Each ctl In Caller.Controls
      If (ctl.ControlType = acLine) And Not ctl.Visible Then
            ' Found an invisible line
        ctl.Visible = True
        Set retVal = ctl
        Exit For
```

```
    End If
Next

Set getFreeLine = retVal

Set retVal = Nothing
Set ctl = Nothing

End Function
```

There are two missing things yet. The first is the function Moved(),
called by an image when it's moved (see clsSlave.mouseMove()). It gets
the index of the moved image as a parameter, and its task is to move all
the lines connected to that image, as they have to follow the image itself.
This is rather easy: it just has to call placeLink() several times, once for
each outgoing edge, passing the array position of the calling (moved)
image as "source," the "other" image array position as "target," and the
correspondent line control:

```
                              CLSMASTER
```

```
Public Sub Moved(ndx As Integer)
' Called by a slave when it's moved
Dim i As Integer

  With Slaves(ndx)
    For i = 1 To UBound(.Edges)
      placeLink ndx, .Edges(i).targetImageNdx, .Edges(i).ctl
    Next
  End With

End Sub
```

And finally, the function placeLink(), which gets the index of the source image, the index of the target image and the line, and uses this line to connect the two images. Does it sound familiar? This function is almost the same as our old Connect(), which we (smartly!) preserved. Let's cut its code and paste it here:

CLSMASTER

```
Private Sub placeLink(src As Integer, tgt As Integer, lin
As Line)
' Resize and position line <lin>
Dim P1 As recPoint, P2 As recPoint

  P1 = obj1.Center()        ' 1
  P2 = obj2.Center()        ' 2

  With lin           ' 3
    .Left = IIf(P1.X < P2.X, P1.X, P2.X)
    .Top = IIf(P1.Y < P2.Y, P1.Y, P2.Y)
    .Width = Abs(P1.X - P2.X)
    .Height = Abs(P1.Y - P2.Y)
    .LineSlant = ((P1.X < P2.X) And (P1.Y > P2.Y)) _
                 Or ((P1.X > P2.X) And (P1.Y < P2.Y))
  End With

End Sub
```

It just needs a few adjustments: modify lines 1 and 2, asking the source and the target objects to tell us the positions of their centers. The line control (line 3) is now called lin, and the rest remains the same:

```
                          CLSMASTER

Private Sub placeLink(src As Integer, tgt As Integer, lin
As Line)
Dim P1 As recPoint, P2 As recPoint

  P1 = Slaves(src).Slave.Center()
  P2 = Slaves(tgt).Slave.Center()

  With lin
    [...]
  End With

End Sub
```

It may be the case to review the whole stuff once more.

The form creates the clsMaster object, passing the four images and creating the links.

In clsMaster, the method Add() adds the images to an array of clsSlave objects so that the dragging is automatically handled. When an image is moved, the involved slave moves the image and then asks the Master (using the provided pointer Locals.Caller) to move all its links.

The whole thing should now work. Run the form, and the four images should move correctly, followed by their linked lines.

How hard is it to add a new link? We just need to add another line to the form, send it to the background, make sure it's invisible, and then create the link, for example, between 1 and 4:

FORM

```
Private Sub Form_Load()
Dim i As Integer

  Set Master = New clsMaster
  Master.Init Me

  For i = 1 To MAX_IMAGES
    Master.Add Me.Controls("imgDrag" & i)
  Next

  Master.createLink 1, 2  ' Link image1 to image2
  Master.createLink 1, 3  ' Link image1 to image3
  Master.createLink 2, 4  ' Link image2 to image4
  Master.createLink 1, 4  ' Link image1 to image4

End Sub
```

That's it. And if we need another image?

Just add the image, and name it `imgDrag5`. Add a couple of invisible lines and send them to the background. In the form, change `MAX_IMAGES` to 5 and create the links we need:

FORM

```
Private Const MAX_IMAGES = 5

Private Master As clsMaster

Private Sub Form_Load()
Dim i As Integer

  Set Master = New clsMaster
  Master.Init Me
```

148

```
For i = 1 To MAX_IMAGES
  Master.Add Me.Controls("imgDrag" & i)
Next

Master.createLink 1, 2   ' Link image1 to image2
Master.createLink 1, 3   ' Link image1 to image3
Master.createLink 2, 4   ' Link image2 to image4
Master.createLink 1, 4   ' Link image1 to image4
Master.createLink 2, 5   ' Link image2 to image5
Master.createLink 4, 5   ' Link image4 to image5

End Sub
```

And it's done.

This case was definitely more complicated, but after all, we had to bypass an Access limitation (or a missing functionality, if you prefer) that is the impossibility to create an array of objects with events. But eventually, we created something generic that works with any number of lines and images, with a minimum number of required changes to the form and the code. You can embed the two classes (and the module) in any of your projects, and they will work (provided you correctly name the images on the form).

What can be done with the things we've seen so far? Just a few examples:

- Funny, colorful interfaces (https://youtu.be/aPtCyNpmErM).

- Different, creative ways to show relations among objects and entities (https://youtu.be/R8CsxiQvs_k).

- Improve the scrolling timeline we're going to build later. We won't do that here, but the objects on the timeline can be made draggable.

But these are really just a drop in the ocean. Your imagination is the limit.

149

4.5. The "Ghost Label" Technique

A variation of this dragging technique can be applied to a label rather than an image to create what I like to call the "ghost label" effect.

This time the hero is not an image but a label. Create a simple form with eight labels, as shown in Figure 4-16.

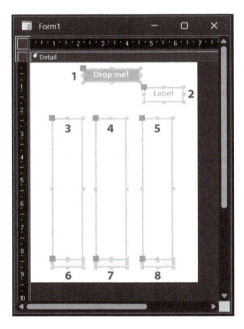

Figure 4-16. *Designing the "ghost label"*

I'll use these names:

```
1 - lbl
2 - lblGhost
3 - lblBase1
4 - lblBase2
5 - lblBase3
```

6 - lblStack1

7 - lblStack2

8 - lblStack3

Labels 3–8 form three sliders, or progress bars, or stacks, or whatever you want to call them.

Then we have the front man in this show, a label simply named lbl, and the main actor, lblGhost. They are all plain labels, there's no trick and no hidden settings, the only thing worth being noticed is that lblGhost is invisible and set to the front.

The effect we want to achieve may be a bit difficult to explain in words. I hope Figures 4-17 to 4-19 can help.

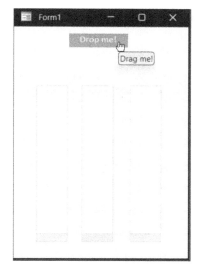

Figure 4-17. *The user "grabs" the top label with the mouse. The "ghost label" appears*

Figure 4-18. *The "ghost" can be dragged*

Figure 4-19. *The "ghost" is dropped in a stack, whose color level increases*

It's a silly example, I know, but it should be enough to understand the potential of this technique.

To start, let's create a brand-new database. We need one single class, name it `clsDraggableLabel`. It's going to be very similar to the first one we wrote, and we could even start from there, as the modifications are not too many. But practice is fundamental, so we are going to rewrite it from scratch. Can you remember how it was?

CLSDRAGGABLELABEL

```
Option Explicit

Private Type recLocals
    dX As Single         ' H position of mouse when drag starts
                         '       (relative to myLabel.Left)
    dY As Single         ' V position of mouse when drag starts
                         '       (relative to
                         '            myLabel.Top)
    formW As Single      ' Container form width
    formH As Single      ' Container form height
    isDragging As Boolean ' TRUE when the user grabs the label
    Ghost As Label       ' The "ghost"
End Type
Dim Locals As recLocals

Private WithEvents myLabel As Label     ' The clickable,
                                        static label
```

There's only one substantial difference with what we did before, a new member: Ghost, the "ghost" label (label 2 in the first picture). Then, of course, we have the clickable label myLabel (label 1 in the first picture), with events, while before we had an image. We already know we can't put it within the structure recLocals (because it's a variable with events), so we declare it outside of it.

Then we have the usual Init() function to collect all the pieces of information we need:

```
                          CLSDRAGGABLELABEL

Public Sub Init(lbl As Label, Ghost As Label, _
                            formW As Single, formH As Single)
    Set myLabel = lbl
    myLabel.OnMouseDown = "[Event Procedure]"
    myLabel.OnMouseMove = "[Event Procedure]"
    myLabel.OnMouseUp = "[Event Procedure]"
    Ghost.Visible = False                            ' 1
    With Locals
        .isDragging = False
        .dX = 0
        .dY = 0
        .formH = formH
        .formW = formW
        Set .Ghost = Ghost                           ' 2
    End With
End Sub

Private Sub Class_Terminate()
    Set myLabel = Nothing
    Set Locals.Ghost = Nothing
End Sub
```

Very similar to our original code but with one more parameter (Ghost) and with two more lines: line 1, to make sure the ghost starts hidden, and line 2, to create a reference to the ghost label on the form. As usual, release the memory when the class terminates.

The mouseDown() event starts as before:

CLSDRAGGABLELABEL

```
Private Sub myLabel_MouseDown(Button As Integer, Shift As
Integer, _ X As Single, Y As Single)
    With Locals
        .isDragging = True
        .dX = X
        .dY = Y
    End With

End Sub
```

But here, we have a relevant difference compared to the original code. When the user grabs the label to move it, the ghost should be made visible and superimposed onto the grabbed label:

CLSDRAGGABLELABEL

```
Private Sub myLabel_MouseDown(Button As Integer, Shift As
Integer, _ X As Single, Y As Single)
    With Locals
        .isDragging = True
        .dX = X
        .dY = Y
    End With

    With Locals.Ghost
        .Move myLabel.Left, myLabel.Top, _
                    myLabel.Width, myLabel.Height      ' 1
        .Caption = myLabel.Caption                     ' 2
```

```
        .BorderStyle = 4                              ' 3
        .Visible = True                               ' 4
    End With

End Sub
```

The ghost is (invisibly) moved and superimposed to the clicked label, copying not only its position and dimensions (line 1) but also its caption (line 2), whatever it is at the moment. We can also add some decorations: we could change the background, the border, the fore color, whatever we want. For example, we can set a dotted border (line 3). At this point, the ghost is ready to be shown (line 4).

What about the mouseMove()? Again, almost identical to our previous version:

```
┌────────────────────────────────────────────────────┐
│                  CLSDRAGGABLELABEL                   │
└────────────────────────────────────────────────────┘
```

```
Private Sub myLabel_MouseMove(Button As Integer, Shift As
Integer, _ X As Single, Y As Single)
    ' The user moves the mouse.
    ' If the image has been grabbed, move it
Dim newX As Single, newY As Single

    Const BORDER = 10        ' Border around the label

    ' Add a tooltip and turn cursor into a hand
    myLabel.HyperlinkSubAddress = myLabel.Caption      ' 1

    With Locals
        If .isDragging Then
                ' HORIZONTAL AXIS
            newX = myLabel.Left + (X - .dX)  ' New label left?
            If (newX < BORDER) Then
```

```
      ' Moving the label way too left
      ' Stop the movement to keep the label within
        the form
    newX = BORDER
ElseIf (newX + myLabel.Width + BORDER > .formW) Then
        ' Moving the label way too right
        ' Stop the movement to keep the label within
          the form
      newX = .formW - BORDER - myLabel.Width
  End If

      ' VERTICAL AXIS
    newY = myLabel.Top + (Y - .dY)
    If (newY < BORDER) Then
      newY = BORDER
    ElseIf (newY + myLabel.Height + BORDER > .formH) Then
      newY = .formH - BORDER - myLabel.Height
    End If

      ' The GHOST label (not the clicked one) moves
    .Ghost.Move newX, newY                            ' 2
    End If
  End With

End Sub
```

I just used the label HyperlinkSubAddress property to add a tooltip
equal to the label caption (line 1). I used this property instead of the more
common ControlToolTip because it also changes the mouse icon to a
hand, which gives the user some visual feedback. The last slight difference
is that though the user clicked on lbl, it's actually Ghost that has to be
moved (line 2).

The mouseUp() is also similar to the original:

CLSDRAGGABLELABEL

```
Private Sub myLabel_MouseUp(Button As Integer, Shift As Integer,
_ X As Single, Y As Single)
    ' The user releases the mouse: stop dragging

  With Locals
    If .isDragging Then
      .isDragging = False
      .Ghost.Visible = False                    ' 1
      myLabel.HyperlinkSubAddress = ""          ' 2
    End If
  End With

End Sub
```

We just need to hide the ghost again (line 1) and reset the cursor (line 2).

Let's stop here for now and switch to the form module. Declare the object (without WithEvents, for now), create the instance in the Form_ Load() event, and destroy it when the form closes:

FORM

```
Option Explicit

Dim obj As clsDraggableLabel

Private Sub Form_Load()
    Set obj = New clsDraggableLabel
    obj.Init Me.lbl, Me.lblGhost, Me.InsideWidth, Me.InsideHeight
End Sub
```

```
Private Sub Form_Close()
  Set obj = Nothing
End Sub
```

If we run the form now, it works more or less as intended. When you click on the label, the ghost label appears (because it's positioned to the front), and the mouseMove() moves it around, and when you release the mouse, it disappears. Now, this thing is fairly useless until we find a way to react to the dropping of the label. We can use an event for this:

CLSDRAGGABLELABEL

```
Option Explicit

Public Event Dropped(X As Single, Y As Single)
```

This is obviously needed in the mouseUp() when the user releases the mouse button:

CLSDRAGGABLELABEL

```
Private Sub myLabel_MouseUp(Button As Integer, Shift As Integer,
_ X As Single, Y As Single)
  With Locals
    If .isDragging Then
      .isDragging = False
      .Ghost.Visible = False
      myLabel.HyperlinkSubAddress = ""
```

```
RaiseEvent Dropped(.Ghost.Left + .dX, .Ghost.Top + .dY)

    End If
  End With
End Sub
```

If you remember, dX and dY are relative to the dragged object left, not to the form, nor to the screen. So .Ghost.Left + .dX is exactly the horizontal position of the mouse, and .Ghost.Top + .dY is its vertical position, both relative to the form top left corner.

Back to the form, we can now declare our object WithEvents:

```
                              FORM

Dim WithEvents obj As clsDraggableLabel
```

And now, we can react to the drop. How? Well, we need to know if the mouse has been dropped within one of the three stacks. So, we'll need a function: let's call it Intersect(), which does the calculation and either returns Nothing, if no pile is hit, or the involved colored label.

```
                              FORM

Private Function Intersect(X As Single, Y As Single) As Label

End Function
```

When we react to the event, the first thing to do is to call this function:

```
                        FORM
```

```
Private Sub obj_Dropped(X As Single, Y As Single)
Dim tgt As Label

   ' Find target stack
   Set tgt = Intersect(X, Y)

End Sub
```

Either tgt is Nothing or is one of the base labels. If this is the case, we increase the height of the colored bar for that pile (e.g., by 1/10 of the whole pile height) and move it upward to simulate the filling:

```
                        FORM
```

```
Private Sub obj_Dropped(X As Single, Y As Single)
Dim tgt As Label

   Set tgt = Intersect(X, Y)

   If Not tgt Is Nothing Then
         ' Increase "filling" label height
      tgt.Height = tgt.Height + lblBase1.Height / 10

         ' Move it upwards to keep bottom alignment
         ' between the base label and the "filling" label
      tgt.Top = tgt.Top - lblBase1.Height / 10
   End If

End Sub
```

Now, the Intersect() function. It takes a point (X, Y) and returns the "filling" label of the stack to which (X, Y) belongs. There are probably several ways to check for this intersection, but we have already a lot to

161

think of, so let's go for a simple, straight, brute-force approach. Since the height is the same for the three stacks, we can just run one check on Y (comparing it to, for example, lblBase1) and then check to which of the three X belongs:

```
                              FORM

Private Function Intersect(X As Single, Y As Single) As Label
    If (Y >= lblBase1.Top) _
              And (Y <= lblBase1.Top + lblBase1.Height) Then

        If (X >= lblBase1.Left) _
              And (X <= lblBase1.Left + lblBase1.Width) Then
                                     Set Intersect = lblStack1
        ElseIf (X >= lblBase2.Left) _
              And (X <= lblBase2.Left + lblBase2.Width) Then
                                     Set Intersect = lblStack2
        ElseIf (X >= lblBase3.Left) _
              And (X <= lblBase3.Left + lblBase3.Width) Then
                                     Set Intersect = lblStack3
        End If

    End If
End Function
```

And here we go. Now, when you drop the ghost out of any base label, nothing happens. But when you drop it within one of the three, another slice of color is added to it.

Of course, there's a million things we can do to make it better. For example, we could animate the stack filling. Update the existing code as follows:

FORM

```
Private Sub obj_Dropped(X As Single, Y As Single)
Dim tgt As Label
Dim i As Single, delta As Single

    Const SPEED = 5        ' Arbitrary speed (pixels/iteration)

    Set tgt = Intersect(X, Y)

    If Not tgt Is Nothing Then

            ' Arbitrary size of color slice increase
        delta = lblBase1.Height / 10

            ' Animate color
        For i = 1 To delta Step SPEED
          tgt.Height = tgt.Height + SPEED
          tgt.Top = tgt.Top - SPEED
          DoEvents
        Next

    End If

End Sub
```

I also added a DoEvents, which is always a good thing to add to a loop that moves things on the form.

Of course, a check on the filling levels is needed for example, when the bases are completely full, it must not be possible to add more color – but that's an easy exercise; the focus of this example was on the drag and drop only.

4.6. Sliding Forms

The dragging engine, especially when joined to the master-slave structure, can be used in many situations, even if several modifications may be required. In this chapter, we'll explore one of these possible variations to create a "sliding forms" effect I used several times in my presentations.

Our goal is to build what is shown in Figure 4-20.

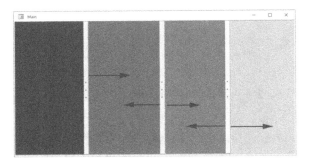

Figure 4-20. *Sliding forms*

In this example, four subforms (but they can be any number) are arranged within a form. A command button is placed between any two forms, acting as a "handle" the user can move (as represented by the blue arrows). The adjacent subforms are resized and repositioned to follow the button movement so that the whole thing appears as a set of sliding windows. The movement of any button is limited by the adjacent button (or the form border).

To give you an idea of the effect, consider Figures 4-21 to 4-23, which show three possible positions of the subforms.

***Figure 4-21.** Sliding forms (example 1)*

***Figure 4-22.** Sliding forms (example 2)*

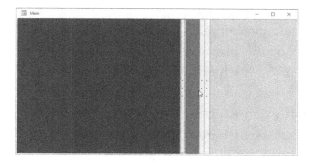

***Figure 4-23.** Sliding forms (example 3)*

Of course, the subforms are fully functional, so it will be possible to place any control on them. This arrangement allows us to show a large amount of data in a very small space.

First, the container form.

In Figure 4-24, the structure has been "expanded" to make it clear how the subforms and the "handles" are placed one after the other. In reality, all of these elements need to be "left aligned" so that there is no space between them. There's no trick here and no hidden settings.

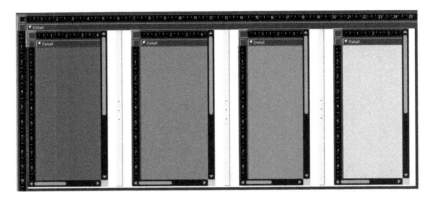

Figure 4-24. *Designing the sliding forms*

The subforms are named smsk1, smsk2, smsk3, and smsk4 for simplicity, but there's no actual need for progressive numbering; they can be named whatever you prefer. Of course, it would also be possible to write some code to automatically align them so that the user could just "drop" them anywhere on the form at design time, and the code would resize and position them properly when the form is loaded. But after all, this should be a rather easy exercise and not strictly related to the actual topic here. So, we'll assume that the subforms and the buttons are already placed and sized correctly at design time.

Then, if we have n subforms, we need n-1 command buttons that are going to be the handles by which the forms are moved. They can have any look and any caption you want, even images if you think it's better, but I prefer to keep them narrow and caption them with a simple dot-dot-dot, Calibri 14, so they have the look you see in the picture. They are named cmdHandle1, cmdHandle2, and cmdHandle3. In this case as well, names are not important, and you can name them as you prefer. I just set their Cursor on Hover property to Hyperlink hand to give the users visual feedback when they hover the mouse over them.

And that's all for the form. Let's move on to the code.

We are going to use a master class (clsHandle_Master) and a slave class (clsHandle_Slave). We already know then that the user will interact with the (single) instance of the master class, which will use the slave class to manage the draggable objects, which, in this case, are neither images nor labels but command buttons. Every instance of clsHandle_Slave should then model one command button. It should sound rather logical, though, that each button is strictly related to the two adjacent subforms, as its movement influences the size and the position of both of them. So, each slave instance will manipulate the three objects (a handle and the two adjacent forms) as a whole.

Let's proceed again with a top-down approach. I want to provide the users with a tool that is as simple as possible. As before, we instantiate and initialize the Master instance in the Form_Load() event and destroy it when the form is closed:

```
                                FORM

Option Explicit

Private Handles As clsHandle_Master

Private Sub Form_Load()
    Set Handles = New clsHandle_Master
    With Handles
        .Init Me

    End With
End Sub
```

```
Private Sub Form_Close()
    Set Handles = Nothing
End Sub
```

Let's add the Init( ) function to the class and postpone its definition for now:

```
                        CLSHANDLE_MASTER

Public Sub Init(Container As Form)

End Sub
```

Then we need a Create( ) function to create a handle object. In our case, we have three of such objects, so we call this function three times. As noted earlier, each instance needs to know the button that will work as a handle and which subform it moves:

```
                            FORM

Private Sub Form_Load()
    Set Handles = New clsHandle_Master
    With Handles
        .Init Me

        .Create cmdHandle1, smsk1, smsk2
        .Create cmdHandle2, smsk2, smsk3
        .Create cmdHandle3, smsk3, smsk4
    End With
End Sub
```

There's only one thing to notice here: the handles must be created from the leftmost to the rightmost; otherwise, what we're doing is not going to work. The master class will manage these objects using an array, assuming the button in slot i is immediately to the left of the button in slot i + 1. If we want to allow them to be created in any order (which should never be the case anyway, I can't see any solid reason for that), more code is needed to check the relative position of each button compared to the others, but that would complicate the code too much.

Let's add Create() to the class:

CLSHANDLE_MASTER

```
Public Function Create(cmdHandle As CommandButton, _
            leftSubform As SubForm, rightSubform As SubForm) _
                                    As clsHandle_Slave

End Function
```

And that's all for the form. From now on, our Master will take care of everything. From the users' point of view, this sliding door thing is extremely simple; the object is just created and initialized (and destroyed).

So, let's focus on the Master.

Similarly to what we did on other occasions, we create a structure to hold the variables we need, that is:

CLSHANDLE_MASTER

```
Option Explicit

Private Type recLocals
    Container As Form
    Handles() As clsHandle_Slave
End Type
Private Locals As recLocals
```

When the class starts, we initialize the array and destroy all the objects when it terminates:

CLSHANDLE_MASTER

```
Private Sub Class_Initialize()
    ReDim Locals.Handles(0)
End Sub

Private Sub Class_Terminate()
Dim i As Integer

    With Locals
        For i = 1 To UBound(.Handles)
            Set .Handles(i) = Nothing
        Next

        Set .Container = Nothing
    End With

End Sub
```

Our Init() function is very simple; it just receives the container form – that's all it needs:

```
                        CLSHANDLE_MASTER

Public Sub Init(Container As Form)
    Set Locals.Container = Container
End Sub
```

Now, Create(), which has to add a new object to the slave array:

```
                        CLSHANDLE_MASTER

Public Function Create(cmdHandle As CommandButton, _
            leftSubform As SubForm, rightSubform As SubForm) _
                                    As clsHandle_Slave
Dim n As Integer

    With Locals
        n = UBound(.Handles) + 1
        ReDim Preserve .Handles(n)
        Set .Handles(n) = New clsHandle_Slave

        Set Create = .Handles(n)
    End With

End Function
```

Now, this object must be initialized somehow. According to what we said discussing the master-slave technique, it needs to receive a pointer to this master class and its position in the array, plus, of course, the button and the two subforms it has to move:

CLSHANDLE_MASTER

```
Public Function Create(cmdHandle As CommandButton, _
            leftSubform As SubForm, rightSubform As SubForm) _
                            As clsHandle_Slave
Dim n As Integer

    With Locals
        n = UBound(.Handles) + 1
        ReDim Preserve .Handles(n)
        Set .Handles(n) = New clsHandle_Slave

        .Handles(n).Init Me, n, cmdHandle, leftSubform,
        rightSubform

        Set Create = .Handles(n)
    End With
End Function
```

Let's now add this Init() function to the slave class. We could use five parameters, but this time, I want to do something different. You probably know this technique, but maybe some of you don't, and it's a good one to know.

CLSHANDLE_SLAVE

```
Public Sub Init(Caller As clsHandle_Master, ParamArray parm())

End sub
```

ParamArray is a VBA word alerting the function that parameters are expected, but their number is not specified at design time. There can be one, two, five, ten, fifty, whatever, but there are rules to follow:

- It can only be used as the last argument in a procedure or function signature.

- It will always be considered as Variant and always byVal (never byRef).

- The array is always zero-based (even when Option Base 1 is specified in the module).

You can pass anything, including objects. BUT if you try to pass an instance of a class, like this Caller here, it will raise an error. And that's why I pass Caller by itself and not in the parameter array. It's a great thing to use when you have a variable number of parameters or when they are too many to be listed one by one.

Since they have no name, it's an extremely good practice to add some comments to the function. In our case:

CLSHANDLE_SLAVE

```
Public Sub Init(Caller As clsHandle_Master, ParamArray parm())
' Parm(0)  Array position
' Parm(1)  Handle button
' Parm(2)  Left subform
' Parm(3)  Right subform

End Sub
```

Now, let's add some local variables to receive all these values. We already know that we also need the main variable, the command button that works as a handle. It's a `WithEvents` variable, so it cannot be included in the structure.

```
                        CLSHANDLE_SLAVE
```

```
Private Type recLocals
    myNdx As Integer                ' Array position of
                                    THIS object

    myParent As clsHandle_Master    ' Pointer to Master class
    myLeft As SubForm               ' Subform to the left of
                                    this handle

    myRight As SubForm              ' Subform to the right of
                                    this handle

    isResizing As Boolean           ' True when dragging
    dX As Single                    ' Mouse position when
                                    drag starts
                                    '      (relative to the
                                    handle <left>)
End Type
Private Locals As recLocals

Private WithEvents cmdHandle As CommandButton
```

These are basically the same variables we used in our original dragging code. Of course, we don't need dY because there will be no movement along the vertical axis.

OK. Now, let's develop our Init(), which is quite simple, just like before. And never forget to release the memory when the class terminates.

```
                        CLSHANDLE_SLAVE
```

```
Public Sub Init(Caller As clsHandle_Master, ParamArray parm())
  Set cmdHandle = parm(1)
  With cmdHandle
    .OnMouseDown = "[Event Procedure]"
    .OnMouseMove = "[Event Procedure]"
    .OnMouseUp = "[Event Procedure]"
  End With

  With Locals
    .myNdx = parm(0)
    Set .myLeft = parm(2)
    Set .myRight = parm(3)
    Set .myParent = Caller
  End With
End sub

Private Sub Class_Terminate()
  Set cmdHandle = Nothing
   With Locals
    Set .myLeft = Nothing
    Set .myRight = Nothing
    Set .myParent = Nothing
  End With
End Sub
```

So far, nothing special. Now, when the user grabs *this* command button with the mouse, the variable .isResizing is set to True to alert the rest of the code about this event, and .dX stores the mouse coordinate relative to the command left position:

```
                    CLSHANDLE_SLAVE
```

```
Private Sub cmdHandle_MouseDown(Button As Integer, _
            Shift As Integer, X As Single, Y As Single)
  With Locals
    .isResizing = True
    .dX = X
  End With

End Sub
```

The mouseMove() starts like the one we wrote in our original dragging code:

```
                    CLSHANDLE_SLAVE
```

```
Private Sub cmdHandle_MouseMove(Button As Integer, _
            Shift As Integer, X As Single, Y As Single)
Dim delta As Single

  With Locals
    If .isResizing Then
        delta = X - .dX

    End If
  End With
End Sub
```

And now, we have a problem. This class doesn't have enough information to move the handle. That's because a handle movement is limited by the position of the previous and the next handles (if any), but an instance of a handle only manages one single command button and doesn't "know" whether other handles exist. Just like before, the Master is the best place to manage the movement, for it holds an array with all the instances (which means buttons and forms) and can access each of them individually. So here, we can't do anything but ask our Master to take care of the movement:

```
                    CLSHANDLE_SLAVE


Private Sub cmdHandle_MouseMove(Button As Integer, _
             Shift As Integer, X As Single, Y As Single)
Dim delta As Single

   With Locals
     If .isResizing Then
        delta = X - .dX

        .myParent.Moved .myNdx, delta
     End If
   End With

End Sub
```

This basically tells the master "Hey, I'm the command button number myNdx, and I've been moved by delta pixels. Do something about it." Let's just note it down for now and postpone the details:

```
                    CLSHANDLE_MASTER


Public Sub Moved(callerNdx As Integer, delta As Single)

End Sub
```

What can we say about the mouseUp()? Nothing special. It just has to communicate that the dragging has stopped, just like the "standard" drag and drop.

```
┌────────────────────────────────────────────────────────────┐
│                    CLSHANDLE_SLAVE                           │
└────────────────────────────────────────────────────────────┘
```

```
Private Sub cmdHandle_MouseUp(Button As Integer, _
              Shift As Integer, X As Single, Y As Single)
   Locals.isResizing = False
End Sub
```

Let's now see what happens in the Moved() method of clsHandle_ Master. This is the core of the whole thing, and unfortunately, it's NOT going to be simple. Let's focus on this sub. A couple of shortcuts may be useful here:

```
┌────────────────────────────────────────────────────────────┐
│                    CLSHANDLE_MASTER                          │
└────────────────────────────────────────────────────────────┘
```

```
Public Sub Moved(callerNdx As Integer, delta As Single)
Dim crtLeft As Single, handleWidth As Single

   With Locals
     crtLeft = .Handles(callerNdx).Left        ' Handle's
                                               current left
     handleWidth = .Handles(callerNdx).Width  ' Handle width

End Sub
```

Before proceeding, let's write these two properties, given their triviality:

```
┌──────────────────────────────────────────────────────────┐
│                    CLSHANDLE_SLAVE                         │
└──────────────────────────────────────────────────────────┘
```

```
Public Property Get Left() As Single
   Left = cmdHandle.Left
End Property

Public Property Get Width() As Single
   Width = cmdHandle.Width
End Property
```

Now, as we said, the movement of the calling handle is limited by the positions of the previous and the next handles, *if* present. We need to find these handles:

```
┌──────────────────────────────────────────────────────────┐
│                    CLSHANDLE_MASTER                        │
└──────────────────────────────────────────────────────────┘
```

```
Public Sub Moved(callerNdx As Integer, delta As Single)
Dim crtLeft As Single, handleWidth As Single
Dim prev As Integer, nxt As Integer

  With Locals
    [...]

    ' Find handle on the left (if any)
    prev = 0
    If (callerNdx > 1) Then prev = callerNdx - 1

    ' Find handle on the right (if any)
    nxt = 0
    If (callerNdx < UBound(.Handles)) Then nxt = callerNdx + 1

End Sub
```

This should be clear. If the caller handle is the leftmost one, it has no previous. Otherwise, the previous is the handle before it in the array. This works because we created the handles from the leftmost to the rightmost if you remember, so that's the order they have in the array.

We do something similar to find the next handle, the one on the right. If the calling handle is the rightmost one, it has no next handle. Otherwise, the next handle is the one that follows in the array.

Now, the new *potential* position for the handle would be crtLeft + delta, but we must first check for its movement limitations. In our basic dragging code, we only had to check this new potential position against the container form boundaries. In this case, we need to compare it to the form *and/or* to another handle position. It's easier if we consider all possible cases separately:

CLSHANDLE_MASTER

```
Public Sub Moved(callerNdx As Integer, delta As Single)
      [...]
   With Locals
        [...]
   newLeft = crtLeft + delta

   If (delta > 0) Then
        ' Moving right
      If (nxt = 0) Then
         ' This is the rightmost handle
         ' Movement limited by the container right border
        If (newLeft + handleWidth > Locals.Container.
        InsideWidth) Then
          newLeft = Locals.Container.InsideWidth - handleWidth
        End If
      Else
```

```
        ' "Internal" handle
        ' Movement limited by the next handle
      With Locals.Handles(nxt)
        If (newLeft + handleWidth >= .Left) Then
          newLeft = .Left - handleWidth
        End If
      End With
    End If
  Else
        ' Moving left
    If (prev = 0) Then
      ' This is the leftmost handle
      ' Movement limited by the container left border
      If (newLeft <= 0) Then newLeft = 0
    Else
      ' "Internal" handle
      ' Movement limited by the previous handle
      With Locals.Handles(prev)
        If (newLeft <= .Left + .Width) Then
          newLeft = .Left + .Width
        End If
      End With
    End If
  End If

End Sub
```

The code should be self-explanatory, and the comments should help
understand it better.

But it's not enough. If we move a handle, we also have to make sure
that its right subform and its left subform are correctly resized and/or
repositioned to stay "attached" to the button.

Let's say I'm moving the second handle (see Figure 4-25), the one pointed at by the blue arrow. It should be obvious that the left (red) subform doesn't actually move. It stays right where it is; its .Left value doesn't change. What changes is its width to follow the movement of the handle.

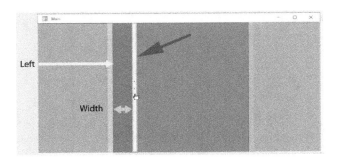

Figure 4-25. *Moving a handle (example 1)*

For the right subform (Figure 4-26, in green), the thing is a bit different. Not only does its width change, but also its .Left coordinate must be modified to make sure its left border follows the movement of the handle (pointed by the blue arrow). It's its *right* border that stays put.

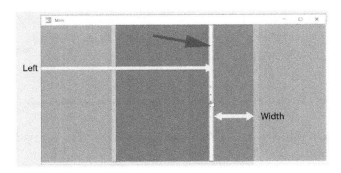

Figure 4-26. *Moving a handle (example 2)*

CLSHANDLE_MASTER

```
Public Sub Moved(callerNdx As Integer, delta As Single)
Dim newLeft As Single
Dim newLeftSubform_Width As Single
Dim newRightSubform_Left As Single
Dim newRightSubform_Width As Single
    [...]

  With Locals
    [...]

    ' Left subform (doesn't move: resize is enough)
    ' ---------------------------------------------
    newLeftSubform_Width = newLeft - _
                .Handles(callerNdx).leftSubform.Left        ' 1

      ' Right subform (move + resize)
      ' ------------------------------
      ' Move
    newRightSubform_Left = newLeft + handleWidth

      ' Resize
    If (nxt = 0) Then
      ' No more handles on the right
      ' The subform extends up to the container border
      newRightSubform_Width = .Container.InsideWidth - _
                                          newRightSubform_Left
    Else
      ' More handles on the right
      ' The subform extends up to the very next handle
      newRightSubform_Width = .Handles(nxt).Left - _
                                          newRightSubform_Left
    End If
End Sub
```

The property on line 1 is missing at the moment; we'll write it in a second. Now, we just have to apply these changes to actually move the objects on the screen:

```
                          CLSHANDLE_MASTER

Public Sub Moved(callerNdx As Integer, delta As Single)
    [...]

  With Locals
    [...]

        ' Move the handle and move/resize the adjacent subforms
    With .Handles(callerNdx)
     .Left = newLeft

     .leftSubform.Width = newLeftSubform_Width

     .rightSubform.Left = newRightSubform_Left
     .rightSubform.Width = newRightSubform_Width
    End With

    DoEvents

  End With
End Sub
```

We add a doEvents to make sure the modifications are applied.

We still need these last three properties. They are straightforward, though:

```
|                                                                    |
|                        CLSHANDLE_SLAVE                             |
|                                                                    |

Public Property Get leftSubform() As SubForm
' Return the left subform
    Set leftSubform = Locals.myLeft
End Property

Public Property Get rightSubform() As SubForm
' Return the right subform
    Set rightSubform = Locals.myRight
End Property

Public Property Let Left(X As Single)
' Return the left position of the handle
    cmdHandle.Left = X
End Property
```

And we're done. When we drag a handle, it moves along with the mouse, and the two adjacent subforms are properly resized. Keep in mind that these are fully functional subforms, so you can add every control you may need.

Is it difficult to add more sliders? Well, no. We just need to resize the form to accommodate one more command button and one more subform. The only code that we need to change is in the Form_Load() event, as we just have to add a .Create call, passing the new elements to the master class. And that's it.

4.7. Conclusion

As you can see, embedding a drag-and-drop engine in your applications is not at all difficult. Just export and import the class (or the classes), and you can immediately transform any image in a draggable object. On some occasions, as we have seen, some adjustments may be needed, but the basic code is always there and always valid.

This is an example of how it can be applied to a ton of different situations. We won't discuss it here, but just to show you what I mean, there is another "famous" interface I made to handle ship deliveries to Ethiopia. Figure 4-27 shows a screenshot from that application.

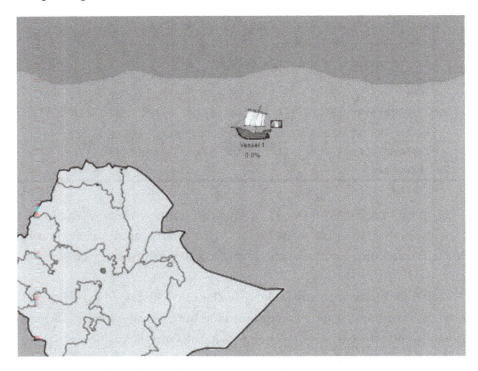

Figure 4-27. *The "Vessel Loader" main form*

The ship on the screen is draggable, but it's made up of four components: the image with the ship, the image with the flag, and the two green labels. All these elements had to be moved together during the dragging, so the basic code had to be modified in a yet different, case-specific way, but the "structure," so to say, was still the same.

Just unleash your imagination!

CHAPTER 5

Advanced Interfaces: Scrollable Timeline

...where we create a scrollable timeline where objects can be placed at run time.

And it's not going to be easy.

In this last chapter, we build a rather complex application: a scrollable timeline where objects can be placed dynamically. Such an object can be very useful in a ton of situations. I first created it when I was consulting for the UN in Ethiopia in 2010–2011 to handle ships and ports, but it can be very handy every time we have to handle events occurring in time. Think, for example, of incoming and outgoing emails, or a set of meetings, or expeditions of goods of any sort, or even incoming and outgoing hotel guests – any situation where we need to provide the users with a visual representation of *temporal* relations among events.

We'll write a class, so this whole timeline engine can be easily imported in any Access project. Building this class is not going to be easy:

- First, we're going to design and build the "physical" timeline on the form, adding the necessary code to make it scrollable.

- After that, we'll use the presence vector technique we discussed in Chapter 3 to place objects on it. This is going to be the hardest part, as it involves a lot of thinking, complex data structures, and many lines of code.

© The Editor(s) (if applicable) and The Author(s),
under exclusive license to APress Media, LLC, part of Springer Nature 2024
A. Grimaldi, *Advanced interactive interfaces with Access*,
https://doi.org/10.1007/979-8-8688-0808-1_5

We have a lot to do, so... let's start!

5.1. Design the Timeline

A lot of work is done on the form. I'll try to illustrate the many parts which makes up our timeline, using several images.

Figure 5-1 shows how the form looks in design mode. As you can see, there are several controls placed on it. The first decision to take is how wide you want the time window to be, that's to say how many days you want to be displayed. I think that 40 is a fair amount, so I placed these 40 labels to hold the day numbers (Figure 5-2).

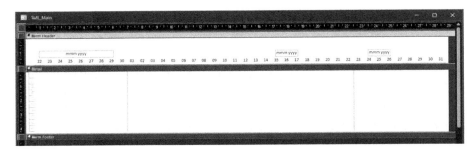

Figure 5-1. *Designing the timeline*

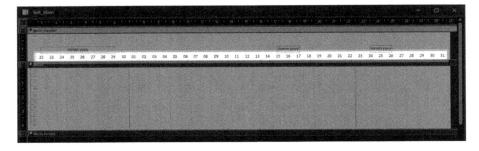

Figure 5-2. *Day placeholders*

In this moment, there are random numbers as placeholders, but they will be changed by the code at run time.

An important role in the process is played by the control names and tags, which will be used in the code to address the single controls. These labels, for example, are named progressively lblDay1, lblDay2, lblDay3, up to lblDay40, and their tags are all set to DAY (Figure 5-3).

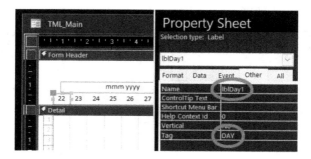

Figure 5-3. *Day placeholders properties*

Forty days can span over three months. That's why we have three labels, named lblMonth1, lblMonth2, and lblMonth3 (Figure 5-4), with a common tag set to MONTH. These labels will show the month and the year of the underlying days.

Figure 5-4. *Month labels*

Again, in this moment, they contain some dummy text as a placeholder, and the actual text (as well as their position and size) will be set at run time.

Then we have the actual timeline. Different "lanes" (Figure 5-5) are necessary because of conflicts when placing the objects. If different objects occupy the same day, they must be placed on different lanes to avoid overlapping. So, a correct estimation of the needed lanes depends on you and the specific situation. In this small-scale example, there are only ten lanes, numbered 1 to 10 using more labels, named lblRowNumber1, lblRowNumber2, lblRowNumber3, up to lblRowNumber10.

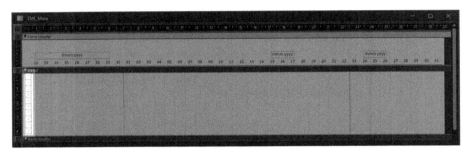

Figure 5-5. *Timeline "lanes"*

Their common tag is ROW_LABEL. Of course, you can add more, or show less, than 10. Useless to say, the more lanes you add, the slower and less smooth the scroll will be.

Then we have some vertical lines that visually separate the days (Figure 5-6).

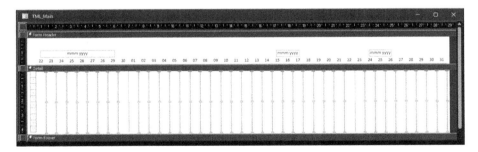

Figure 5-6. *Day separators*

In principle, they are not strictly necessary, but I think they provide the user with a valuable visual reference. Their names are not important, but their tags have been set to DAY_SEPARATOR.

Finally, as an additional visual cue, we have two bolder vertical lines named linMonthSeparator1 and linMonthSeparator2, and the tag is not used (Figure 5-7). As we said, with 40 visible days, we can have a maximum of three different months shown at the same time, so two separators are enough.

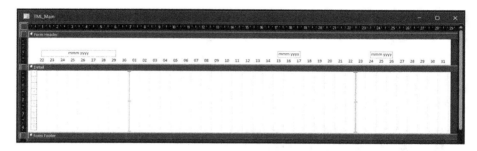

Figure 5-7. *Month separators*

Again, these two lines have no functional role but provide a visual cue to the user.

5.2. Make It Scrollable

OK, this is the design of the form. Now, as I said, the code is going to be rather complex, so let's try to keep it (at least) easy to modify and maintain. This goal can be achieved defining some constants, to be used in the code, holding the names of the involved controls. Let's create a code module and write the following:

```
[CODE MODULE]
```

Option Explicit

```
' Timeline extension
Public Const MIN_DATE = #1/1/2024#
Public Const MAX_DATE = #12/31/2024#

' "Today" formatting
Public Const TODAY_BACKCOLOR = 13017476      ' RGB(132,161,198)
Public Const TODAY_FORECOLOR = vbWhite

' Control name prefixes
Public Const MONTH_SEPARATOR = "linMonthSeparator"
Public Const MONTH_LABEL = "lblMonth"
Public Const DAY_LABEL = "lblDay"
Public Const ROW_LABEL = "lblRowNumber"
```

The first two constants define the timeline boundaries. We can use them to limit the timeline to a specific time frame, if needed. If the timeline doesn't need to be limited, they can be set to whatever date you prefer, according to your machine limitations on dates, for example, from #1/1/1900# to #12/31/2900#. In our case, the timeline will be limited to the year 2024.

Then we have the back color and the fore color of the day label that represents "today." I want "today" to be highlighted if it's visible on the screen, and this is my choice of color: a white text on a pale blue background, so it will look like .

Then there is the name prefix of the two vertical lines that separate the months; then the three month name labels on the top, the 40 day labels, and the 10 lane numbers.

Should we decide to change the names of any set of controls, we can simply change the constant values here, without a global "find and replace," which is always a potentially dangerous operation, and leave the rest of the code untouched. In addition, this application may be used by other people who may want or may need to name the controls differently, and this section would be a huge help for them, especially if they are not acquainted with the rest of the code.

Now, it should be clear that this is all about day intervals, so an "interval" is our fundamental piece of information, and we need a way to model it. What is a date interval? Well, it's a simple object: there's a starting date and an ending date. A structure seems, again, our best choice. It obviously must be a *public* structure since it's likely to be needed in many parts of the application, including the class we're about to write. We can once more use the "companion module" concept, consciously breaking the isolation/encapsulation OOP paradigm. And the module we just created is a perfect candidate, so let's save it as mdlTimeline and add the structure definition:

```
                          MDLTIMELINE


Public Type recDateInterval
  firstDate As Long
  lastDate As Long
  Duration As Integer
End Type
Public TML As clsTimeline
```

Of course, .Duration is a bit redundant, as it can be calculated every time it's needed as the difference between the two dates, but it's easier to calculate it only once, when .firstDate or .lastDate change, and have it available anytime. As always, a bit of redundancy is acceptable, if it can simplify some operations.

We name TML the (public) instance that represents our timeline. And this module for now is done.

Let's go back to the form for a moment, which of course has to create the instance of the class in its Form_Load() event and destroy it when it closes:

FORM

```
Option Explicit

Private Sub Form_Load()
  Set TML = New clsTimeline
  TML.Init Me
End Sub

Private Sub Form_Unload(Cancel As Integer)
  Set TML = Nothing
End Sub
```

As usual, the class will need an Init() function, which receives the form on which the timeline is defined, to extract all the information it needs.

Note that since we defined TML as Public, we can only have one timeline in our project, linked to one specific form. But if we have more timelines scattered on different forms, there's nothing wrong in creating several (independent) instances of the class, one per form. The only difference, of course, is that the declaration of the public instance must be removed from the module, and each form will declare its own:

[EACH FORM MODULE]

Option Explicit

Private TML as clsTimeline

The rest of the code will remain the same.

That's all for the form, and we're ready to start with the real work: the timeline class. Luckily, we won't need to apply the master-slave technique, as we'll only need one class. Create a class module and name it clsTimeline. We'll need some local variables to describe the geometry of our timeline and to handle the scroll. Guess what – I'll use a structure:

CLSTIMELINE

Option Explicit

Private Type recLocals
  timelineForm As Form
  visibleDays As Integer
  maxMonths As Integer
  dayWidth As Integer
  laneCount As Integer
  timelineWindow As recDateInterval
End Type
Private Locals As recLocals

- timelineForm is clearly a pointer to the container form.

- visibleDays holds the number of visible days.

- `maxMonths` is the (max) number of visible months, which is actually a bit redundant as it can be somehow inferred by the number of visible days. But there's no reason to complicate our lives more than needed.

- `dayWidth` is the width of a single day label, since they all have the same width, or which is the same, the distance between two vertical lines.

- `laneCount` is the number of lanes in our timeline (in our example, 10).

- `timelineWindow` holds the visible dates, that's to say the visible portion of the timeline. In other words, 40 days, between `MIN_DATE` and `MAX_DATE`, are currently shown. In the rest of the chapter, we'll call this interval the *visible timeline*. So, its `.firstDate` component will be the first visible day (i.e., the date in `lblDay1`), `.lastDate` will be the last visible date (i.e., the date in `lblDay40`), and `.Duration` will always be 40.

The values of most of these variables are actually known from the very beginning. We already know that `visibleDays=40`, `maxMonths=3`, and so on. But if we decide to change the timeline layout, adding/removing lines or columns, or changing the day label width, we should also change the code, and this is always a potentially dangerous operation. So, we'll have the code count and calculate all these numbers at run time. This way, at the cost of adding this bunch of more variables, we'll be free to play with the timeline without having to worry about the code.

We start with the `Init()` function called by the `Form_Load()` event. We use this function to collect information about the controls on the calling form:

```
                          CLSTIMELINE
```

```
Public Sub Init(callerForm As Form)
Dim ctl As Control

  With Locals
    Set .timelineForm = callerForm                  ' 1

    .visibleDays = 0
    .maxMonths = 0
    .dayWidth = 0
    For Each ctl In .timelineForm.Controls
        Select Case ctl.Tag
          Case "ROW_LABEL"                           ' 2
            ' Lane count
            .laneCount = .laneCount + 1

          Case "DAY"                                 ' 3
            ' Visible days count and day width
            .visibleDays = .visibleDays + 1
            .dayWidth = ctl.Width

          Case "MONTH"                               ' 4
            ' Max visible months
            .maxMonths = .maxMonths + 1
        End Select
      Next
  End With

  Set ctl = Nothing

  ' Go to "today" as a starting point
  gotoDate Date                                      ' 5

End Sub
```

```
Private Sub Class_Terminate()
  Set Locals.timelineForm = Nothing
End Sub
```

First, we store a reference to the calling form itself (line 1). Then, we use the names and the tags of the controls to get information about the geometry of the timeline: so, we start a loop on all the controls of the form and check for the current control tag:

- If we meet a lane label (line 2), we increment the lane count by 1 (at the end, it will be 10, in our example).

- If we meet a day label (line 3), we increment the visible day count by 1 (it will be 40 at the end), and we also use this control to determine the "width" of a day, that is, the distance between two days.

- Finally, if we meet a month separator (line 4), we increase the count of the visible months (it will be 3 at the end). Note that this number is *not* the count of the months currently shown but the *maximum* number of months that can be shown at the same time.[1]

We close this function moving the timeline to the current date (line 5), so to give the user a starting point. And, as usual, we release the memory when the class terminates.

Ok, now the goToDate() function. It's not so simple as one may hope for because there are several checks that need to be performed.

---

[1] I hope this is clear: with 40 visible days, for example, two OR three months may be shown, depending on the first visible day: .MaxMonths will be 3 anyway.

First, let's remove the color from today's label. That's because if "today" is currently shown, the correspondent label is colored. But when this function is called, the visible timeline jumps to a different set of 40 days, where "today" may not be visible. Its label must then be reset to the default colors:

```
                        CLSTIMELINE
```

```
Public Sub gotoDate(dt As Long)
  colorToday False
End Sub

Private Sub colorToday(isColored As Boolean)

End Sub
```

We'll write colorToday() later.

First (obvious) check: the specified date must be within the timeline boundaries.

```
                        CLSTIMELINE
```

```
Public Sub gotoDate(dt As Long)
  colorToday False

  If (dt < MIN_DATE) Then dt = MIN_DATE
  If (dt > MAX_DATE) Then dt = MAX_DATE
End Sub
```

Now, by design, we decide to place the selected date *at the center* of the timeline, so around the 20th day label, one more, one less. Of course, this is not possible when the selected date is too close to the first or to the last date. If the first date (MIN_DATE) is the 1st of January and we want to go to the 9th, the 9th can't be placed in the center, as there wouldn't be enough days to fill the left half of the timeline. In this case, we force MIN_DATE to be the first visible date. The same happens on the other side if the chosen date is too close to MAX_DATE: we force MAX_DATE to be the last visible date. Don't forget, though, that .firstDate and .lastDate in our recDateInterval structure are strictly connected by the number of visible days: so, when we change one, we also have to adjust the other (of course .Duration never changes, as there are always 40 days shown).

This can be translated into VBA as follows:

CLSTIMELINE

```
Public Sub gotoDate(dt As Long)
  colorToday False
  If (dt < MIN_DATE) Then dt = MIN_DATE
  If (dt > MAX_DATE) Then dt = MAX_DATE

  With Locals
    If (dt - MIN_DATE + 1 < .visibleDays \ 2) Then
      ' <dt> is too close to MIN_DATE
      ' Show MIN_DATE as first date
      .timelineWindow.firstDate = MIN_DATE
      .timelineWindow.lastDate = MIN_DATE + .visibleDays - 1
    ElseIf (MAX_DATE - dt + 1 < .visibleDays \ 2) Then
      ' <dt> is too close to MAX_DATE
      ' Show MAX_DATE as last date
      .timelineWindow.lastDate = MAX_DATE
      .timelineWindow.firstDate = MAX_DATE - .visibleDays + 1
    Else
      ' <dt> can be centered
      .timelineWindow.firstDate = dt - .visibleDays \ 2 + 1
```

```
        .timelineWindow.lastDate = .timelineWindow.firstDate + _
                                    .visibleDays - 1
      End If
    End With
End Sub
```

Having updated the visible window boundaries, we can redraw the timeline, so all the captions will be updated:

CLSTIMELINE

```
Public Sub gotoDate(dt As Long)

  [...]

  With Locals
    [...]
    Redraw
  End With

End Sub
```

Let's focus on this Redraw() function:

CLSTIMELINE

```
Private Sub Redraw()

End Sub
```

There are many possible strategies to follow to redraw the timeline. I opted for a procedure that probably is not the best, in terms of performance, but with the advantage of being rather straightforward.

To start, I hide those controls whose presence is not guaranteed, as it depends on the visible time window. This includes the vertical month separators, which are one less than the potentially visible months. We don't know how many months are displayed – there might be one month only, if the user designed the timeline with less than 30 days. So maybe even the first line must be hidden:

CLSTIMELINE

```
Private Sub Redraw()
Dim m As Integer

  With Locals
    With .timelineForm
      ' Month separators
      For m = 1 To (Locals.maxMonths - 1)
        .Controls(MONTH_SEPARATOR & m).Visible = False
      Next

End Sub
```

See how our choice of the control names, using progressive numbering, again simplifies this part of the code.

Now, the top month labels, which show the month names. The only thing we can be sure about them is that *one* will always be visible because we're showing at least one day on the timeline. So, we can hide them starting from the second:

CLSTIMELINE

```
Private Sub Redraw()
Dim m As Integer

  With Locals
    With .timelineForm
      [...]

      For m = 2 To Locals.maxMonths
        .Controls(MONTH_LABEL & m).Width = 0
      Next
    End With

End Sub
```

Why do I set their width to 0, rather than making them invisible? That's because when the timeline is redrawn, their width will have to be changed anyway because of the scroll. They have to "cover," so to say, the visible days of the month they refer to. So, it makes no sense to also hide them, as I would have to set them visible again, and that would be an additional, useless, and time-consuming operation.

Now, the first problem is to detect which fractions of months are visible, because, as we said, we must correctly place the month labels (Figure 5-8), each one spanning from the first to the last *visible* day of each month. We need to know the first and the last date for each visible month. We use an array to store these dates.

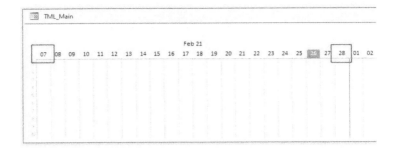

Figure 5-8. *First and last month dates*

CLSTIMELINE

```
Private Sub Redraw()
Dim m As Integer
Dim monthLimits() As recDateInterval

  With Locals
    [...]

    ReDim monthLimits(.maxMonths)
    m = 1

End Sub
```

Of course, the first month starts with the first visible day on the timeline, so:

```
                        CLSTIMELINE
```

```
Private Sub Redraw()
[...]

  With Locals
    [...]
    monthLimits(1).firstDate = .timelineWindow.firstDate
End Sub
```

Now, let's scan all the 40 days that will be shown and take proper actions for each of them:

```
                        CLSTIMELINE
```

```
Private Sub Redraw()
[...]
Dim d As Byte, crtDate As Long

  With Locals
    [...]

    For d = 0 To (.visibleDays - 1)
      crtDate = .timelineWindow.firstDate + d
End Sub
```

We need to do several things:

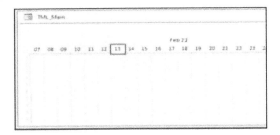

1. Update the caption of the label corresponding to crtDate.

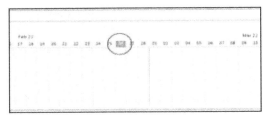

2. Apply the highlight if crtDate is today.

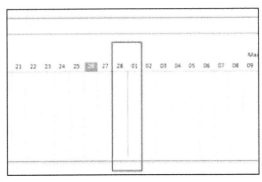

3. Show the vertical month separation if crtDate is the first day of a month.

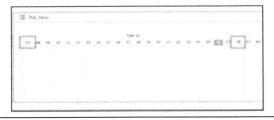

4. Update the array monthLimits() to store the first and the last visible day of each month.

(*continued*)

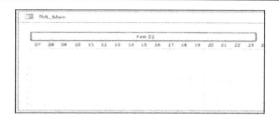

5. Use this information to properly resize and caption the month name labels.

A lot of things! Let's start:

1. *Update the caption of the label corresponding to crtDate.*
   We need to know in which label crtDate must be shown. We'll write a function (getDateLabelByPos()), which takes a number between 1 and 40 and returns the correspondent day label:

CLSTIMELINE

```
Private Function getDateLabelByPos(n As Integer) As Label

End Function
```

Now, update the caption of this label:

CLSTIMELINE

```
Private Sub Redraw()
[...]

  With Locals
    [...]
```

```
For d = 0 To (.visibleDays - 1)
  crtDate = .timelineWindow.firstDate + d

  With getDateLabelByPos(d + 1)
    .Caption = Format(crtDate, "dd")

End Sub
```

2. *Apply the highlight if crtDate is today.*

```
CLSTIMELINE
```

```
Private Sub Redraw()
[...]

  With Locals
    [...]

    For d = 0 To (.visibleDays - 1)
      crtDate = .timelineWindow.firstDate + d

      With getDateLabelByPos(d + 1)
        .Caption = Format(crtDate, "dd")
        If (crtDate = Date) Then colorToday True

End Sub
```

We already mentioned colorToday(); we'll write it later.

3. *Show the vertical month separation if crtDate is the
   first day of a month.*

   If crtDate starts a month, we show the vertical
   month separator. We move it five pixels before the
   vertical day separator to make it more visible:

```
┌──────────────────────────────────────────────────────────────┐
│                          CLSTIMELINE                           │
└──────────────────────────────────────────────────────────────┘
```

```
Private Sub Redraw()
[...]

  With Locals
    [...]

    For d = 0 To (.visibleDays - 1)
      crtDate = .timelineWindow.firstDate + d

      With getDateLabelByPos(d + 1)
        .Caption = Format(crtDate, "dd")
        If (crtDate = Date) Then colorToday True
        If (Day(crtDate) = 1) Then
          Locals.timelineForm.Controls(MONTH_SEPARATOR &
          m).Left = _.Left - 5
          Locals.timelineForm.Controls(MONTH_SEPARATOR &
          m).Visible = _True
        End If
      End With
End Sub
```

4. *Update the array monthLimits() to store the first and the last visible day of each month.*

   If crtDate is the first day of a new month, this means that the previous date was the last day of the current month. If, on the other hand, crtDate is the last visible day of the timeline, then crtDate itself is the last visible day of its month because there are no more days to show:

CLSTIMELINE

```
Private Sub Redraw()
[...]

  With Locals
    [...]

    For d = 0 To (.visibleDays - 1)
      [...]

      If (Day(crtDate) = 1) Then
        ' If <crtDate> starts a new month,
        ' the previous date was the last day of the
          current month
        monthLimits(m).lastDate = crtDate - 1
      ElseIf (crtDate = .timelineWindow.lastDate) Then
        ' Same if <crtDate> is the last visible day
        monthLimits(m).lastDate = crtDate
      End If

End Sub
```

---

5. *Use this information to properly resize and caption the month name labels.*

So, if we have closed a month, we have its first and its last visible day, and we can correctly resize and place the label with its name. Then we are ready to start a new month:

```
┌─────────────────────────────────────────────────────┐
│                    CLSTIMELINE                        │
└─────────────────────────────────────────────────────┘
```

```
Private Sub Redraw()
[...]

  With Locals
    [...]

    For d = 0 To (.visibleDays - 1)
      [...]

      If (Day(crtDate) = 1) Or (crtDate = .timelineWindow.
      lastDate) Then
          ' If a month has just finished
          ' or the last visible day is reached (truncated month)
          ' we can size and place the month label
        With .timelineForm.Controls(MONTH_LABEL & m)

          .Caption = Format(crtDate - 1, "mmm yy")
            ' e.g. "Mar 22"

          .Left = getDateLabelByPos(monthLimits(m).firstDate _
                          - Locals.timelineWindow.firstDate
                          + 1).Left
          ' Left aligned with the day label
          '       corresponding to this month's first day
          '       (offset from the first visible day)

          .Width = (monthLimits(m).lastDate - _
                  monthLimits(m).firstDate + 1) * Locals.
                  dayWidth
            ' Number of visible days in this month * width of
            one day label
        End With
```

```
      ' If a month has just finished, a new month is starting
      If (Day(crtDate) = 1) Then
        m = m + 1
        monthLimits(m).firstDate = crtDate
      End If
    End If
  Next
End With

DoEvents                              ' 1
End Sub
```

At the end, we add DoEvents (line 1). This DoEvents is crucial because this Redraw() function will be called several times a second when the timeline is scrolling: without it, the system might look frozen, as it is too busy handling the timeline redraw, which is a heavy task in case there are many lanes and objects, and the process would only "unfreeze" when a timeline boundary is reached or the user stops scrolling. This might not happen when the timeline is small like this one, depending on your computer capacities, in which case the DoEvents might be useless.

The core is done. We still need a couple of ancillary functions. Let's start with getDateLabelByPos(), which is quite easy. As we said, it gets a number (in our example, between 1 and 40) and returns the correspondent day label:

```
CLSTIMELINE
```

```
Private Function getDateLabelByPos(n As Integer) As Label
Dim retVal As Control

  Set retVal = Nothing
```

```
If (n >= 1) And (n <= Locals.visibleDays) Then          ' 1
  Set retVal = Locals.timelineForm.Controls(DAY_LABEL & n)  ' 2
End If

Set getDateLabelByPos = retVal
Set retVal = Nothing
End Function
```

I added an additional check (line 1) to make sure the number is actually within the visible timeline so that it's possible to find the label. Line 2 takes advantage of the way we named the labels, with a prefix (stored in the constant DAY_LABEL) followed by a number.

Then we need colorToday(). It basically has to apply or remove the highlight colors from today's label. The operation is complicated by two facts: first, "today" might be out of the visible timeline. Second, if it's visible, it can be any of the 40 day labels, so we have to find it:

```
                          CLSTIMELINE
```

```
Private Sub colorToday(isColored As Boolean)
  If isVisible(Date) Then                                 ' 1
    With getDateLabelByDate(Date)                         ' 2
      If isColored Then
        If (.ForeColor <> TODAY_FORECOLOR) Then
          .ForeColor = TODAY_FORECOLOR
        End If
        If (.BackColor <> TODAY_BACKCOLOR) Then
          .BackColor = TODAY_BACKCOLOR
        End If
      Else
        If (.ForeColor <> vbBlack) Then .ForeColor = vbBlack
```

```
        If (.BackColor <> vbWhite) Then .BackColor = vbWhite
      End If
    End With
  End If
End Sub
```

isVisible() on line 1 is another function that returns True if the specified date is within the visible timeline, False otherwise. getDateLabelByDate() (line 2) is a new function too, which takes a date and returns the correspondent label. We need this new function because the one we already have is based on a *position*, not a *date*.

The rest of the code should be straightforward. Just notice the presence of redundant Ifs to avoid applying unneeded changes, thus slightly speeding up the execution and reducing the annoying flickering of the affected controls, typical of how Access handles the screen updates.

There are two more functions to write, but they are extremely simple:

```
                          CLSTIMELINE
```

```
Public Function isVisible(dt As Long) As Boolean
  isVisible = (dt >= Locals.timelineWindow.firstDate) _
                        And (dt <= Locals.timelineWindow.
                        lastDate)
End Function

Private Function getDateLabelByDate(dt As Long) As Label
Dim n As Integer

  ' Offset from the first day label
  n = DateDiff("d", Locals.timelineWindow.firstDate, dt) + 1
  Set getDateLabelByDate = getDateLabelByPos(n)

End Function
```

`isVisible()` is very straightforward; it just checks if the specified date is within the visible timeline. I make it `Public` because it may be a useful function for the users, so they will be able to call it from the form.

`getDateLabelByDate()` takes the distance between the specified date and the first visible day, and that's the position of the label we're looking for. We then use the other function (`getDateLabelByPos()`) to retrieve it.

Wow! It's been quite a ride, but if you made everything right, now the timeline is correctly drawn. Save and run the form: "Today" is highlighted in the center of the visible timeline, and the 40 days are correctly shown. The month labels are correctly centered upon "their" dates.

We can also play a bit with it. Since we made `TML` public, we can use it in the Immediate Window. For example, let's jump to another date:

```
tml.goToDate #25 Oct#
```

Figure 5-9 shows the result: the date we chose is centered in the timeline.

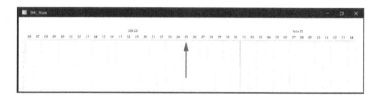

Figure 5-9. *Centered date*

Let's try with a date close to the absolute first date, which is 1st of January:

```
tml.goToDate #5 Jan#
```

As you can see in Figure 5-10, since it's not possible to center this date, the timeline goes as far as possible, that's to say `MIN_DATE`.

Figure 5-10. *Date too close to the timeline start*

On the other side:

```
tml.goToDate #25 Dec#
```

Again (Figure 5-11), the requested date can't be centered, so the last day is set to MAX_DATE.

Figure 5-11. *Date too close to the timeline end*

5.3. Add Navigation Controls

Now, let's add some controls to make the timeline scrollable (Figure 5-12).

Figure 5-12. *Navigation controls*

The leftmost one, cmdFirst, jumps to the first available date. Remember, we created two constants, MIN_DATE and MAX_DATE, which delimit the time frame. cmdFirst will jump to MIN_DATE.

Similarly, the rightmost button, cmdLast, will move the visible timeline to show MAX_DATE. The other two buttons, cmdPrev and cmdNext, will scroll the timeline one day at a time, back or forward.

We want some requirements to be matched:

- The scroll must be continuous: if I keep the mouse button down on cmdPrev or cmdNext, the timeline must keep scrolling one day at a time until I release the button or until a timeline boundary is reached.

- The buttons that are not applicable must be disabled. For example, when I click on cmdFirst and jump to the timeline start, that button and cmdPrev become useless and must be disabled, following the "good practices" we discussed in the first chapter.

First of all, let's update our module. Following the convention we described earlier, let's add the names of the movement buttons, so if I decide to change them, I will just have to modify these lines:

```
                              MDLTIMELINE

Option Explicit

[...]

Public Const CMD_PREVIOUS_NAME = "cmdPrev"
Public Const CMD_NEXT_NAME = "cmdNext"
Public Const CMD_FIRST_NAME = "cmdFirst"
Public Const CMD_LAST_NAME = "cmdLast"
```

Back to our class module. In the local structure, we'll need another variable, a Boolean, which is somehow like the variable isDragging we used in the drag-and-drop engine:

CLSTIMELINE

```
Option Explicit

Private Type recLocals
  timelineForm As Form
  visibleDays As Integer
  maxMonths As Integer
  dayWidth As Integer
  laneCount As Integer
  timelineWindow As recDateInterval
  isScrolling As Boolean
End Type
Private Locals As recLocals
```

Of course, the four buttons we added must respond to some events, so we need to declare them as WithEvents objects. We then use the Init() sub to initialize these objects and to make them responsive to the events we need:

CLSTIMELINE

```
Option Explicit
[...]

Private WithEvents cmdFirst As CommandButton
Private WithEvents cmdPrev As CommandButton
Private WithEvents cmdNext As CommandButton
```

218

```vb
Private WithEvents cmdLast As CommandButton

Public Sub Init(callerForm As Form)
[...]

  With Locals
    [...]

    Set cmdFirst = .timelineForm.Controls(CMD_FIRST_NAME)
    With cmdFirst
      .OnClick = "[Event Procedure]"
    End With

    Set cmdPrev = .timelineForm.Controls(CMD_PREVIOUS_NAME)
    With cmdPrev
      .OnMouseDown = "[Event Procedure]"
      .OnMouseUp = "[Event Procedure]"
    End With

    Set cmdNext = .timelineForm.Controls(CMD_NEXT_NAME)
    With cmdNext
      .OnMouseDown = "[Event Procedure]"
      .OnMouseUp = "[Event Procedure]"
    End With

    Set cmdLast = .timelineForm.Controls(CMD_LAST_NAME)
    With cmdLast
      .OnClick = "[Event Procedure]"
    End With
  End With

  Set ctl = Nothing

  [...]

End Sub
```

Note that cmdFirst and cmdLast just need to react to a simple click, while cmdPrev and cmdNext must be "continuous" buttons, meaning that they are activated by a mouseDown event, and stop their action only when the user releases the mouse button – which is a mouseUp event.

As usual, don't forget to release these objects when the class terminates:

```
                        CLSTIMELINE

Private Sub Class_Terminate()
  Set Locals.timelineForm = Nothing
  Set cmdFirst = Nothing
  Set cmdPrev = Nothing
  Set cmdNext = Nothing
  Set cmdLast = Nothing
End Sub
```

Now, the code for cmdFirst and cmdLast is trivial. We already have a function, gotoDate(), which jumps to a specific date. All we have to do is to pass MIN_DATE and MAX_DATE to it:

```
                        CLSTIMELINE

Private Sub cmdFirst_Click()
  gotoDate MIN_DATE
End Sub

Private Sub cmdLast_Click()
  gotoDate MAX_DATE
End Sub
```

And that's it. We can already test it. Save and run the form, and see how clicking these buttons brings you right to the boundaries of the timeline.

The code for the other two buttons is slightly more complex but still quite straightforward. Let's take care of cmdPrev first. When the button is pressed, the timeline should scroll backward by one single day. We need a variable to store the current first visible date:

CLSTIMELINE

```
Private Sub cmdPrev_MouseDown(Button As Integer, Shift As
Integer, _ X As Single, Y As Single)
' Scrolls one day backward
Dim newFirst As Long

End Sub
```

Now, when the button is pressed the first visible date is

CLSTIMELINE

```
Private Sub cmdPrev_MouseDown(Button As Integer, Shift As
Integer, _ X As Single, Y As Single)
Dim newFirst As Long

    With Locals
      newFirst = .timelineWindow.firstDate
    End With

End Sub
```

Here, we also have to register the event that the scrolling has begun, as the mouse button is down. We use the Boolean variable we defined earlier:

CLSTIMELINE

```
Private Sub cmdPrev_MouseDown(Button As Integer, Shift As
Integer, _ X As Single, Y As Single)
Dim newFirst As Long

  With Locals
    newFirst = .timelineWindow.firstDate
    .isScrolling = True
  End With

End Sub
```

Then, as long as the button remains pressed, we scroll backward one day at a time:

CLSTIMELINE

```
Private Sub cmdPrev_MouseDown(Button As Integer, Shift As
Integer, _ X As Single, Y As Single)
Dim newFirst As Long

  With Locals
    newFirst = .timelineWindow.firstDate
    .isScrolling = True
```

```
Do While .isScrolling
  newFirst = newFirst - 1
  gotoDate newFirst + .visibleDays \ 2 - 1
Loop
End With

End Sub
```

Remember that gotoDate() (which "virtually" moves the timeline) tries to center the date passed as a parameter and ends with a call to Redraw() (which "physically" moves the timeline). So, at every iteration of this loop, the timeline is actually scrolled on the screen (by one day).

When does it stop? Well, either when MIN_DATE has been reached or when the user releases the button. The first case is handled by gotoDate() itself, if you remember. For the second case, we use the button's mouseUp() event:

```
CLSTIMELINE
```

```
Private Sub cmdPrev_MouseUp(Button As Integer, Shift As
Integer, _ X As Single, Y As Single)
  Locals.isScrolling = False
  DoEvents
End Sub
```

The loop in cmdPrev_MouseDown() (driven by .isScrolling) is canceled. We add a doEvents to make sure the instruction is executed even when the mouse button is still pressed.

Let's test it, starting with a single click on the button (which may be difficult since the timeline is "light" and the whole loop takes a tiny fraction of second). The timeline should go one day back in time. In this case, the mouseDown() sets .isScrolling to True, the loop is executed, and the timeline is shifted and redrawn. The mouseUp() sets .isScrolling to False, and the loop doesn't have the time to be executed again.

Now, let's keep the mouse down for a while. In this case, .isScrolling remains True, and the loop is executed more than once. When the mouse is released, .isScrolling becomes False and the loop stops.

The code for the other button, cmdNext, is almost the same, and we can copy and paste what we have already written for its companion, cmdPrev:

```
                            CLSTIMELINE

Private Sub cmdNext_MouseDown(Button As Integer, Shift As
Integer, _ X As Single, Y As Single)
' Scrolls one day forward
Dim newFirst As Long

  With Locals
    newFirst = .timelineWindow.firstDate
    .isScrolling = True

    Do While .isScrolling
      newFirst = newFirst + 1                        ' 1
      gotoDate newFirst + .visibleDays \ 2 - 1
    Loop
  End With

End Sub
```

```
Private Sub cmdNext_MouseUp(Button As Integer, Shift As
Integer, _ X As Single, Y As Single)
  Locals.isScrolling = False
  DoEvents
End Sub
```

The only (obvious) difference is the plus sign on line 1.

And we're done. Save and run, and all the four buttons should work properly. Also, notice how "today" gets highlighted as long as it is within the visible window.

There's only one more thing we have to do, and it's the visual feedback to the user. We said we want the buttons to be disabled when they can't be used. So, we'll write one more function that will assess the situation and enable/disable the buttons accordingly. What's the best place to call this function? In my opinion, it's gotoDate(). It is called every time there is a movement, even from the Init() function, and it's the place where the new boundaries of the visible timeline are defined. So, after the timeline has been updated by calling Redraw(), let's also update the command buttons. Name it enableAll():

```
                        CLSTIMELINE
```

```
Public Sub gotoDate(dt As Long)

    [...]
    Redraw
    enableAll
  End With

End Sub
```

This new function is somehow more complex than we could think. The problem is that it is called every time the timeline is redrawn. So, during a continuous scroll, it can be called several times each second. We can't just blindly enable an already enabled button or disable an already disabled button. These operations take time, slow down the process, and most of all produce a quite annoying flashing of the involved controls. We can partially solve these problems adding some redundant Ifs:

```
                            CLSTIMELINE
```

```
Private Sub enableAll()
Dim isOn As Boolean

  With Locals
    isOn = (MIN_DATE < .timelineWindow.firstDate)
    If isOn Then
      If Not cmdFirst.Enabled Then cmdFirst.Enabled = True
      If Not cmdPrev.Enabled Then cmdPrev.Enabled = True
    Else
      If cmdFirst.Enabled Then cmdFirst.Enabled = False
      If cmdPrev.Enabled Then cmdPrev.Enabled = False
      .isScrolling = False
    End If

    isOn = (.timelineWindow.lastDate < MAX_DATE)
    If isOn Then
      If Not cmdNext.Enabled Then cmdNext.Enabled = True
      If Not cmdLast.Enabled Then cmdLast.Enabled = True
    Else
      If cmdNext.Enabled Then cmdNext.Enabled = False
      If cmdLast.Enabled Then cmdLast.Enabled = False
```

```
      .isScrolling = False
   End If
End With

End Sub
```

The strategy is rather clear: isOn is True if there are days to scroll to, so the corresponding button should be enabled. Both buttons are enabled or disabled only if they are not already in that target state. If there are no more days to scroll to, then we reached an edge of the timeline. The actual scrolling has already been stopped by goToDate(), so here, we just have to set .isScrolling to False so that the loop in the mouseDown() event is not executed anymore.

And this is all. As you can see, if you run the form, when we reach the beginning of the timeline, the left buttons are disabled and are enabled again as soon as we scroll right. Same on the right side, when the end of the timeline is reached.

And now we have a fully dynamic, scrollable timeline.

5.4. Placing Objects

Building the timeline was the easiest part. Now, previously, we discussed the "bit-field" technique, and the whole thing may have been a bit cumbersome to some of you, but at the end of the day, we created a class that can be used in any project. We have now a chance to see a practical application: we're going to embed this class in our timeline project and modify it to match our needs in this specific case. Unfortunately, this is going to be the most complicated part of the whole process.

Back to our Access file. So far, we have our timeline form, the timeline class, and the "companion" code module with some constants and the main data structure, recDateInterval. The first thing we want to do is to import our clsVector.

227

Now, we need to add some labels to the timeline, which we're going to use as objects (Figure 5-13). For this example, just a few will be enough.

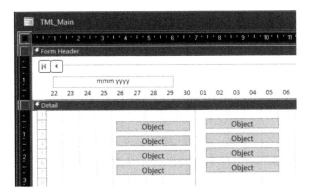

Figure 5-13. *"Object" labels*

Format them as you prefer. In this example (Object is just a dummy caption to have an idea of the final look), I gave them a black fore color and a green background and a thin dark gray border. The caption is centered, and the font size is 9 points. Their names are not important, but I want their tags to be OBJECT (this will simplify our code), and they must start as invisible, so at design time, you can place them wherever you prefer. Their actual size and position will be calculated at run time.

Now, to start, I'm going to do something I discussed in the first chapter: I will get rid of the Date data type. We have used the Date data type a few times in our code, and I did it because we were already doing strange things and I didn't want to introduce another element of perplexity. But now, before starting this last and more complex part, I prefer to switch to a more comfortable environment, so to say.

As I said, I don't like the Date data type, with all its issues in terms of localization and null values. I definitely prefer to replace it with Long (in our case, as we are only dealing with dates, not times; otherwise, Single would be better). No more nulls, no more format problems and ambiguity, easy (numeric!) comparisons between dates, and so on. So, what I'll do here is to globally replace As Date with As Long, and in the rest of the code, I will always use Long instead of Date.

For the moment, nothing else changes in clsVector and mdlGeneral, and nothing changes in the form code. All modifications will occur in clsTimeline.

Now, the first thing we need to do is model the objects that we place on the timeline. An array seems to be a reasonable structure to hold them all. But for each of them, we have to store several properties: the caption, the lifespan (that's to say the starting date and the duration), the "physical" label control on the form, and the timeline lane where the label will be placed. All these pieces of information can be packed, as usual, in a UDT, which makes their handling easier. Not enough, though. We also need another array, which models the lanes on the timeline. And here is where our new class plays its role. So, the final data structure looks like:

CLSTIMELINE

```
Option Explicit

Private Type recObjects
  Caption As String
  Lifespan As recDateInterval
  myLabel As Label
  myLane As Integer
End Type
Private Objects() As recObjects

[...]
```

We'll soon get into more details about the role of clsVector in the management of this Lanes() array, but for now, just declare it.

As usual, we can use the existing Init() function to initialize these new arrays. If you remember, the form with the timeline calls this function on its Form_Load() event, and among other things, we also count the available lanes. Now we can use this information to correctly size our Lanes() array:

CLSTIMELINE

```
Public Sub Init(callerForm As Form)
    ' Collects information on the "physical" timeline
    ' (<callerForm> controls)
Dim ctl As Control
Dim i As Integer, j As Integer

  With Locals
  [...]      ' <-- The code in here counts the available lanes

    ' Init Lanes()
    ReDim Lanes(.laneCount, DateDiff("m", MIN_DATE, MAX_
    DATE) + 1)
    For i = 1 To UBound(Lanes, 1)
      For j = 1 To UBound(Lanes, 2)
        Set Lanes(i, j) = New clsVector
      Next
    Next

  End With

  ReDim Objects(0)

  [...]

End Sub
```

So, what is this Lanes() exactly? It's a bidimensional array (see Figure 5-14), which somehow mimics the timeline. The *whole* timeline, not just the visible part. There are .laneCount rows (in our example, only 10, because we designed a timeline with ten rows), and a number of columns matching the number of months between MIN_DATE and MAX_DATE. Remember that these are the dates we set as boundaries for our timeline. In our specific example, we defined MIN_DATE to be January 1st and MAX_DATE to be December 31st, so we have 12 columns.

	Month 1	Month 2	Month 3	.....	Month 12
Lane 1					
Lane 2					
Lane 3				......	
⋮	⋮	⋮	⋮		⋮
Lane 10					

Figure 5-14. *Graphical representation of the "lanes"*

Of course, it's possible to dynamically "expand" this array to accommodate objects out of the current date range, but as I said, this is just a simplified example, and we already have too many things to think of.

Each element of this array is an instance of clsVector. Now, when we built clsVector, we created an enumeration of masks, enmVectorMasks. We needed it because we wanted to use this class *per se*, but in this timeline context, we don't need it any longer, as we need *dynamic* masks calculated and modified at run time. So, just remove the enumeration from the class, and replace all its occurrences with a simple Long. As we said, a Long has 32 bits, and since no month has more than 31 days, it's the perfect candidate for our presence vectors.

The role of these numbers in Lanes() should be clear: each bit of each number represents a day of the corresponding month, on the corresponding lane. We'll set it to 1 if that day on that lane is occupied by an object, and we'll set it to 0 otherwise. Figure 5-15 shows the initial situation, with all vectors set to 0.

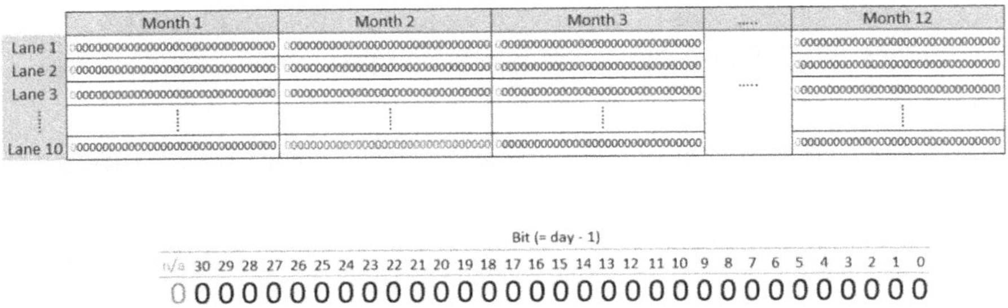

	Month 1	Month 2	Month 3	.....	Month 12
Lane 1	00000000000000000000000000000	00000000000000000000000000000	00000000000000000000000000000		00000000000000000000000000000
Lane 2	00000000000000000000000000000	00000000000000000000000000000	00000000000000000000000000000		00000000000000000000000000000
Lane 3	00000000000000000000000000000	00000000000000000000000000000	00000000000000000000000000000	.....	00000000000000000000000000000
⋮	⋮	⋮	⋮		⋮
Lane 10	00000000000000000000000000000	00000000000000000000000000000	00000000000000000000000000000		00000000000000000000000000000

Bit (= day - 1)

n/a 30 29 28 27 26 25 24 23 22 21 20 19 18 17 16 15 14 13 12 11 10 9 8 7 6 5 4 3 2 1 0

0 0 0 0 0 0 0 0 0 0 0 0 0 0 0 0 0 0 0 0 0 0 0 0 0 0 0 0 0 0 0 0

Figure 5-15. *Exploding the bit vectors*

The last bit (bit 31) of each mask will never be used, but this is not a problem. Note that the days are represented in reversed order: day 1 is represented by bit 0, which is to the *right* of the bit representation. This may be a bit confusing, but it's just a convention. Day n is then represented by bit n -1. If you prefer, you can consider day 1 associated with bit 30, in which case, day n would be associated with bit 31 - n. But this would require several changes in our code and calculations, and I feel more comfortable with the first solution. After all, it's just a matter of habit.

So, how can the calling form ask for a new object to be placed? We can write a function, say, addObject():

CLSTIMELINE

```
Public Sub addObject(objName As String, startDate As Long, _

                                  duration As Integer)

End Sub
```

It will take the object name (which will be used to caption the label) and its starting date (as a Long), and we can choose to pass its duration or its end date. I prefer to use the duration.

This function is going to be the focus point of this part: most of the new things will happen here. So be aware, this is NOT going to be simple.

To start, of course, we add the new object to the Objects array:

```
CLSTIMELINE
```

```
Public Sub addObject(objName As String, startDate As Long, _
                                          duration As Integer
  ReDim Preserve Objects(UBound(Objects) + 1)

  With Objects(UBound(Objects))
    .Caption = objName
    With .Lifespan
      .firstDate = startDate
      .duration = duration
      .lastDate = .firstDate + .duration - 1
    End With

  End With
End Sub
```

OK, this was easy, but now the hard part begins. We have to find a place on the timeline for this object. We need the following pieces of information:

- Which days the object occupies, month by month

- Which lane can host the object, avoiding conflicts with other, already existing objects

To solve these problems, we need several additional variables and structures. First of all, we need to know which months are involved in this object placement. We can build a function, say, clipInterval(), that goes like this:

```
                          CLSTIMELINE
```

```
Private Function clipInterval(interval1Start As Long, _
                 interval1End As Long, _
                 interval2Start As Long, _
                 interval2End As Long) As recDateInterval

End Function
```

It takes two date intervals and clips one against the other, returning a date interval. Let's use it to determine the intersection between this new object's lifespan and the timeline:

```
                          CLSTIMELINE
```

```
Public Sub addObject(objName As String, startDate As Long, _

                                      duration As Integer)
Dim clipped As recDateInterval

  ReDim Preserve Objects(UBound(Objects) + 1)

  With Objects(UBound(Objects))
    .Caption = objName
    With .Lifespan
      .firstDate = startDate
      .duration = duration
      .lastDate = .firstDate + .duration - 1
    End With
```

```
    clipped = clipInterval(.Lifespan.firstDate, .Lifespan.
    lastDate, _
                              MIN_DATE, MAX_DATE)

  End With
End Sub
```

Now, let's extract the first month and the last month of this intersection:

| CLSTIMELINE |

```
Public Sub addObject(objName As String, startDate As Long, _
                                duration As Integer)
Dim clipped As recDateInterval
Dim firstMonthNdx As Integer, lastMonthNdx As Integer

    [...]

    clipped = clipInterval(.Lifespan.firstDate, .Lifespan.
    lastDate, _
                MIN_DATE, MAX_DATE)
    firstMonthNdx = DateDiff("m", MIN_DATE, clipped.
    firstDate) + 1
    lastMonthNdx = DateDiff("m", MIN_DATE, clipped.
    lastDate) + 1

  End With
End Sub
```

Note that these two values are not dates but simple integers, offsets from the timeline start: this means that if we consider the first month of the (whole) timeline as month number 1, then the object starts in month number firstMonthNdx and ends in month number lastMonthNdx.

For example (Figure 5-16), if MIN_DATE is January and the object starts in April, firstMonthNdx will be 4 (January, February, March, April).

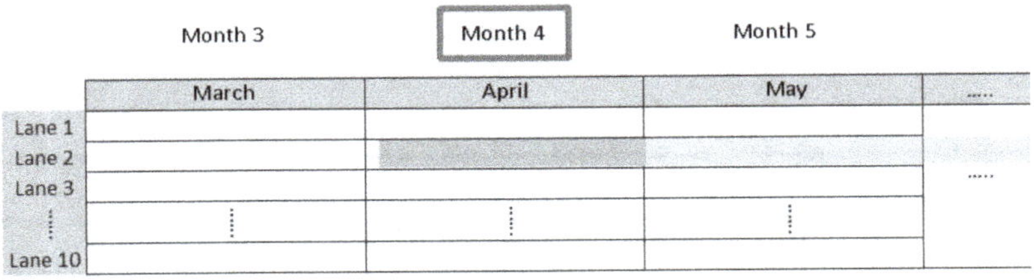

Figure 5-16. *Object example (starting month)*

Similarly (Figure 5-17), if MIN_DATE is January and the object ends in May, lastMonthNdx will be 5 (January, February, March, April, May).

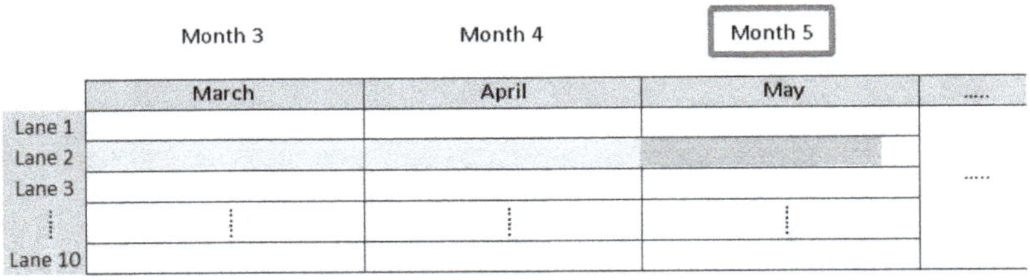

Figure 5-17. *Object example (ending month)*

We can now use these numbers to calculate the intersections between the object and each month in between. We'll store these numbers in an array, objMonthDays():

```
┌─────────────────────────────────────────────────────┐
│                    CLSTIMELINE                        │
└─────────────────────────────────────────────────────┘

Public Sub addObject(objName As String, startDate As Long, _
                                    duration As Integer)
Dim clipped As recDateInterval
Dim firstMonthNdx As Integer, lastMonthNdx As Integer
Dim m As Integer
Dim objMonthDays() As recDateInterval

    [...]

    ReDim objMonthDays(firstMonthNdx To lastMonthNdx)
    For m = firstMonthNdx To lastMonthNdx

    Next
  End With
End Sub
```

Let's focus on a single month m. Remember that m is actually just an offset from the timeline start, so which month is it actually? This is easy:

```
┌─────────────────────────────────────────────────────┐
│                    CLSTIMELINE                        │
└─────────────────────────────────────────────────────┘

Public Sub addObject(objName As String, startDate As Long, _
                                    duration As Integer)
Dim crtMonth As Long

    [...]

    ReDim objMonthDays(firstMonthNdx To lastMonthNdx)
    For m = firstMonthNdx To lastMonthNdx
      crtMonth = DateAdd("m", m - 1, MIN_DATE)
```

```
    Next
  End With
End Sub
```

With this operation, we transform the month offset into a proper date. Using a normal `DateSerial()`, we can find this month's first and last day:

CLSTIMELINE

```
Public Sub addObject(objName As String, startDate As Long, _
                                          duration As
                                          Integer)
Dim crtMonth As Long
Dim crtMonthFirstDay As Long, crtMonthLastDay As Long

    [...]

    ReDim objMonthDays(firstMonthNdx To lastMonthNdx)
    For m = firstMonthNdx To lastMonthNdx
      crtMonth = DateAdd("m", m - 1, MIN_DATE)
      crtMonthFirstDay = DateSerial(Year(crtMonth),
      Month(crtMonth), 1)
      crtMonthLastDay = DateSerial(Year(crtMonth), _
                                   Month(crtMonth) + 1, 0)

    Next
  End With
End Sub
```

Nothing special, this is a standard way in VBA to get the first and the last day of a month.

Now, we must calculate the intersection of our object with the current month m. The function clipInterval() can help us again:

CLSVECTOR

```
Public Sub addObject(objName As String, startDate As Long, _
                                       duration As Integer)

    [...]

    ReDim objMonthDays(firstMonthNdx To lastMonthNdx)
    For m = firstMonthNdx To lastMonthNdx
      crtMonth = DateAdd("m", m - 1, MIN_DATE)
      crtMonthFirstDay = DateSerial(Year(crtMonth), _
                                      Month(crtMonth), 1)
      crtMonthLastDay = DateSerial(Year(crtMonth), _
                                     Month(crtMonth) + 1, 0)
      objMonthDays(m) = clipInterval(.Lifespan.firstDate, _
                                     .Lifespan.lastDate, _
                                     crtMonthFirstDay, _
                                     crtMonthLastDay)

    Next
  End With
End Sub
```

Here, we are intersecting the object's entire lifespan with the current month only. At the end of the loop, we finally know which days this object occupies in each month of its lifespan. Let's make a practical example (Figure 5-18).

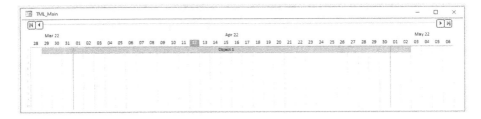

Figure 5-18. *Placing an object*

If our object starts on March 29th and ends on May 2nd, our loop variable m goes from 3 (March) to 5 (May).

For m = 3 (March), we get

- crtMonth = 3 (actually, #1 March#, but just focus on the month number)

- crtMonthFirstDay = #1 March#

- crtMonthLastDay = #31 March#

- objMonthDays(3).StartDate = #29 March#

- objMonthDays(3).EndDate = #31 March#

On the second iteration, for m = 4 (April), we get

- crtMonth = 4 (actually, #1 April#, but just focus on the month number)

- crtMonthFirstDay = #1 April#

- crtMonthLastDay = #30 April#

- objMonthDays(4).StartDate = #1 April#

- objMonthDays(4).EndDate = #30 April#

And on the third and last iteration, for m = 5 (May), we get

- crtMonth = 5 (actually, #1 May#, but just focus on the month number)

- crtMonthFirstDay = 1 May#

- crtMonthLastDay = #31 May#

- objMonthDays(5).StartDate = #1 May#

- objMonthDays(5).EndDate = #2 May#

Now, we want to use our bit-field technique to handle this information. To do so, we must calculate some proper masks for the months "touched" by the current object. We could do this in the same loop we just wrote, but I prefer to keep this part separate to make the code more readable, so we'll write a separate function:

```
                        CLSTIMELINE
```

```
Private Function buildMask(startAt As Integer, _
                            duration As Integer) As Long
End Function
```

This buildMask() function takes the object starting day (a number between 1 and 31) for a certain month, and a number of days, and returns a proper mask (that's to say a Long number), where every bit corresponding to an occupied day is set to 1 and all the others are set to 0. This is why, at the very beginning, we deleted the enumeration in clsVector: we don't need that static set of masks; we need to calculate a new mask dynamically, every time an object is added to the collection.

Let's create a vector to temporarily store the masks we are building for this object, say, objectMasks(). Each item in this vector (one per month) will be an instance of clsVector. We set up a loop from the first to the last involved month. For each, we create an instance of the vector class and give it a value depending on the days occupied by the object in that month (which we have just calculated and stored in objMonthDays()), using our new buildMask():

```
                          CLSTIMELINE
```

```
Public Sub addObject(objName As String, startDate As Long, _
                                         duration As Integer)

Dim objectMasks() As clsVector

    [...]

    ReDim objectMasks(firstMonthNdx To lastMonthNdx)
    For m = firstMonthNdx To lastMonthNdx
      Set objectMasks(m) = New clsVector
      objectMasks(m).Reset buildMask(Day(objMonthDays(m).
      firstDate), _
                objMonthDays(m).duration)

    Next

  End With
End Sub
```

OK, this was the hardest part. Now, we have a set of masks, one for each month in the object's lifespan, which tell us which days are needed to place it, month by month. What we have to do now is to find an available lane for the object: a lane where all these days are free, not occupied by any other objects. Basically, we need to compare these object masks with the timeline masks, (Lanes()) lane by lane, month by month, and see if we can find a free spot. If we find it, we can place the object there:

CLSTIMELINE

```
Public Sub addObject(objName As String, startDate As Long, _
                                        duration As Integer)
Dim crtLane As Integer, isOK As Boolean

    [...]

    crtLane = 1                                    ' 1
    Do
        isOK = True                                ' 2

        For m = firstMonthNdx To lastMonthNdx      ' 3
            isOK = isOK And Not Lanes(crtLane,
            m).isOn(objectMasks(m).Value)
        Next

        If Not isOK Then crtLane = crtLane + 1      ' 4
    Loop Until isOK Or (crtLane > Locals.laneCount) ' 5

    End With
End Sub
```

So, what's going on here? We start examining Lane 1 (line 1). isOK (line 2) is a variable that is True if we find a suitable lane, so the loop can exit, and that's its default value.

We can use crtLane if and only if it can accommodate *all* of the object masks for its *whole* lifespan (firstMonthNdx to lastMonthNdx), and that's what the loop (line 3) tries to assess. Remember that the class method isOn() checks whether a mask is already contained in the specified vector. If not, then crtLane has enough room in month m, and we can use it to accommodate that month segment of the object. The loop continues checking the other months of the object's lifespan. If isOK remains True, then we have found a place for our object. If those days on that lane are

243

already occupied by another object, isOK becomes False: in this case, we try the very next lane (line 4).

The loop goes on until we find an empty lane, or we run out of lanes (line 5). So, if we exit the loop with isOK = False, then all the available lanes have at least one of the needed segments occupied, and there's no place for our object. At least, we should inform the user with a message box, but that's not relevant here. If, on the other hand, isOK = True, then we have found a suitable lane, and we can assign it to the object. In this case, we also have to update the lane masks; as those days are now occupied, so we have to mark them as no longer available to other objects:

CLSTIMELINE

```
Public Sub addObject(objName As String, startDate As Long, _
                                    duration As Integer)

    [...]

    If isOK Then
        ' Assign the found lane to the object
        .myLane = crtLane

        ' Update all lanes
        ' adding this object's masks to each lane+month mask
        For m = firstMonthNdx To lastMonthNdx
            Lanes(crtLane, m).maskAdd objectMasks(m).Value
        Next
    Else
        MsgBox "Can't place this object"
    End If

    End With
End Sub
```

Finally, we have to draw the object on the timeline, *if necessary*. Let's use another function for this, say, drawObject(). "If necessary" is needed because the object may or may not be within the visible timeline. When it's not, objMonthDays(m).Duration are all 0, but we haven't checked for this situation yet, to keep the code simpler. We'll give this task to this new function. Also, never forget to clear the memory before exiting:

```
┌──────────────────────────────────────────────────────────┐
│                       CLSTIMELINE                          │
└──────────────────────────────────────────────────────────┘

Public Sub addObject(objName As String, startDate As Long, _
                                        duration As Integer)

    [...]

    drawObject UBound(Objects)

    ' Clear memory
    For m = firstMonthNdx To lastMonthNdx
      Set objectMasks(m) = Nothing
    Next

  End With
End Sub

Private Sub drawObject(ndx As Integer)

End Sub
```

We have some functions to write. The first one is clipInterval(), which intersects two dates. Now, there are several ways to calculate a date intersection. I opted for a brutal force approach. Perhaps not elegant, perhaps not the shortest, but very clear to understand and rather quick to execute. I simply consider all the possible combinations. If no intersection is found, the function will return a duration of 0.

This is the logic behind the code:

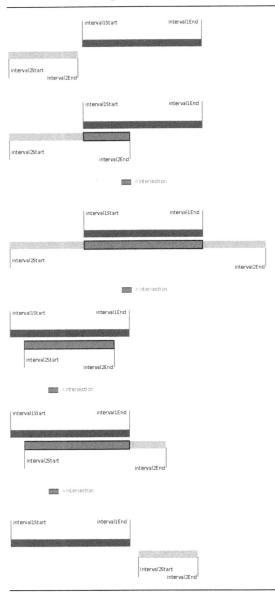

If the second interval ends before the first starts, then there is no intersection.

If the second interval starts before the first interval and ends within it, then the intersection is [interval1Start, interval2End].

If the second interval completely embeds the first, then the intersection is the first interval itself.

If the first interval completely embeds the second, then the intersection is the second interval itself.

If the second interval starts within the first and ends with or after it, then the intersection is [interval2Start, interval1End].

If the second interval starts after the end of the first, there is no intersection.

246

With this approach, the final function is rather straightforward:

```
                          CLSTIMELINE
```

```
Private Function clipInterval(interval1Start As Long, _
                  interval1End As Long, _
                  interval2Start As Long, _
                  interval2End As Long) As recDateInterval
Dim retVal As recDateInterval

  retVal.duration = 0
  If (interval2Start < interval1Start) Then
    If (interval2End < interval1Start) Then
      GoTo exitMe
    ElseIf (interval2End <= interval1End) Then
      retVal.firstDate = interval1Start
      retVal.lastDate = interval2End
    Else
      retVal.firstDate = interval1Start
      retVal.lastDate = interval1End
    End If
  ElseIf (interval2Start <= interval1End) Then
    If (interval2End <= interval1End) Then
      retVal.firstDate = interval2Start
      retVal.lastDate = interval2End
    Else
      retVal.firstDate = interval2Start
      retVal.lastDate = interval1End
    End If
  Else
    GoTo exitMe
  End If
```

```
  retVal.duration = retVal.lastDate - retVal.firstDate + 1

exitMe:
  clipInterval = retVal
```

```
End Function
```

Let's now write the `buildMask()` function, which takes a day of a month and a number of days and returns a proper mask. We need one additional notion of binary arithmetic: multiplying a binary number by 2 means shifting all the bits of its binary representation to the left by one position. For example, 20 is 00010100, so 40 is 00101000. Keep this in mind while we write this function.

What does "proper mask" mean? Let's make an example. Say that we call the function with `startAt` = 5 and `duration` = 3. This means that our object starts on day 5 and lasts three days. Then, the value we're looking for is:

Bit 32	Bit 31	...	Bit 7	Bit 6	Bit 5	Bit 4	Bit 3	Bit 2	Bit 1	Bit 0
N/A	Day 31		Day 8	Day 7	Day 6	Day 5	Day 4	Day 3	Day 2	Day 1
0	0	...	0	1	1	1	0	0	0	0

In other words, 1110000. Let's start by building a (binary) number with a 1 for each day of `duration`:

CLSTIMELINE

```
Private Function buildMask(startAt As Integer, _
                                     duration As
Integer) As Long
Dim retVal As Long
Dim i As Integer

  retVal = 1

  For i = 1 To (duration - 1)
    retVal = retVal * 2 + 1
  Next

End Function
```

I'll try to clarify this step. Imagine the duration is 3. We're starting with retVal = 1. Let's visualize it using only three bits for simplicity:

> 001

In the first iteration of the loop, retVal is first multiplied by 2, which gives (as we said earlier)

> 010

and then it's increased by 1, which gives

> 011

The net result of the first iteration is a number with two bits set to 1. The second (and last) iteration does the same operations, ending up with

> 111

which is exactly what we wanted: a binary number with as many 1s as the value of duration. Note that the longest month is 31 days, and the Long data type has 32 bits, so there is no risk of overflowing during the left shifting.

This number is the left part of our mask. Now we have to add "enough 0s," which in this case means 3, as we saw before. How can we add the 0s? Well, according to the binary arithmetic, just like we did a moment ago, we can multiply by 2 "enough" times so that the leftmost 1 falls on startAt:

CLSTIMELINE

```
Private Function buildMask(startAt As Integer, _
                                    duration As

Integer) As Long
Dim retVal As Long
Dim i As Integer

  retVal = 1

  For i = 1 To (duration - 1)
    retVal = retVal * 2 + 1
  Next

  For i = 1 To (startAt - 1)
    retVal = retVal * 2
  Next

  buildMask = retVal

End Function
```

At each iteration, retVal (which starts with its current value of 111) is multiplied by 2, shifting its bits one place to the left. Suppose startAt is 5, then the loop is repeated four times, and retVal ends up being

    1110000

And this is the proper mask for an object starting on day 5 and lasting three days.

Last step: drawObject(). The basic idea is to assign one label to each object, position it, and show it. But we can't simply assign a new label to each object we create, because the available labels are limited, and there might be more objects than labels. We need to manage them wisely. What we can do is assign a label to an object when it needs to be drawn and take it back when it goes outside the visible timeline, so the same label can be made available again for another object.

In detail, this is what we need to do:

1. If O is inside the visible timeline
2.   If it doesn't have a label, then assign it a label
3.   Set label position and size, and show it
4. Else (object must not be shown)
5.   If it has a label, reclaim it
6. End If

Let's examine each single step:

1. If O is inside the visible timeline

This is easy, as we already have a suitable function:

CLSTIMELINE

```
Private Sub drawObject(ndx As Integer)
Dim clipped As recDateInterval

  With Objects(ndx)
    clipped = clipInterval(.Lifespan.firstDate, .Lifespan.
    lastDate, _
    Locals.timelineWindow.firstDate, Locals.timelineWindow.
    lastDate)

  End With

End Sub
```

The object is inside the visible timeline (so it must be drawn) if
`clipped.Duration` is not 0:

```
CLSTIMELINE
```

```
Private Sub drawObject(ndx As Integer)
Dim clipped As recDateInterval

  With Objects(ndx)
    clipped = clipInterval(.Lifespan.firstDate, .Lifespan.
    lastDate, _
    Locals.timelineWindow.firstDate, Locals.timelineWindow.
    lastDate)
    If (clipped.duration > 0) Then

    End If
  End With

End Sub
```

2. If it doesn't have a label, then assign it a label

We have to make sure the object has an associated label:

```
CLSTIMELINE
```

```
Private Sub drawObject(ndx As Integer)
Dim clipped As recDateInterval

  With Objects(ndx)
    clipped = clipInterval(.Lifespan.firstDate, .Lifespan.
    lastDate, _
    Locals.timelineWindow.firstDate, Locals.timelineWindow.
    lastDate)
```

```
    If (clipped.duration > 0) Then
        If .myLabel Is Nothing Then
          Set .myLabel = assignLabel()
          If .myLabel Is Nothing Then Exit Sub
          .myLabel.Caption = .Caption
        End If
    End If
  End With

End Sub

Private Function assignLabel() As Label

End Function
```

We'll later write the function assignLabel(), which returns an available label. If the function returns Nothing, then there are no more free labels on the form, and the whole procedure gracefully exits just by skipping this object. Of course, this part should be more elaborated, as the user needs to be alerted that there are no more available labels, but this is something not really interesting in our discussion. If the label is found, its caption is set.

3. Set label position and size, and show it

To correctly place this object on the assigned lane, we first need to know the position of the day label corresponding to its starting date. We already have a function for that:

CLSTIMELINE

```
Private Sub drawObject(ndx As Integer)
Dim clipped As recDateInterval
Dim lblDay As Label
```

```
With Objects(ndx)
  clipped = clipInterval(.Lifespan.firstDate, .Lifespan.
  lastDate, _
  Locals.timelineWindow.firstDate, Locals.timelineWindow.
  lastDate)
  If (clipped.duration > 0) Then
    If .myLabel Is Nothing Then
      Set .myLabel = assignLabel()
      If .myLabel Is Nothing Then Exit Sub
      .myLabel.Caption = .Caption
    End If
```

Set lblDay = getDateLabelByDate(clipped.firstDate)

```
  End If
End With
```

```
End Sub
```

lblDay (Figure 5-19) is the base to correctly place the label. In fact, it gives the label's left position. But we can also add a small, arbitrary margin for aesthetical reasons.

Figure 5-19. *Object starting day*

```
margin = lblDay.Width \ 20 l = lblDay.Left + margin
```

The object width (Figure 5-20) is also easy to find: it's the width of one day multiplied by the visible duration (in days) of the object, minus the right and left margins.

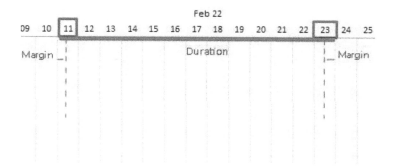

Figure 5-20. *Object duration*

```
w = lblDay.Width * clipped.duration - (2 * margin)
```

The top position of the object (Figure 5-21) is the top of the assigned lane, which is the same as the top of the corresponding lane label, and its height is obviously the height of the lane label.

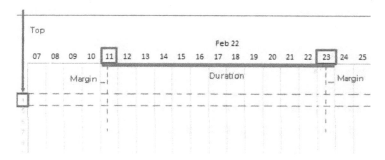

Figure 5-21. *Object top*

```
t = Locals.timelineForm.Controls(ROW_LABEL & .myLane).Top
h = Locals.timelineForm.Controls(ROW_LABEL & .myLane).Height
```

We have now everything we need, so we can finally place and size the object and show it (if you remember how we built the timeline, all labels are hidden when the form is opened). And don't forget to clear the memory before leaving:

```
CLSTIMELINE
```

```
Private Sub drawObject(ndx As Integer)
Dim clipped As recDateInterval
Dim lblDay As Label
Dim margin As Long
Dim l As Long, w As Long, t As Long, h As Long

  With Objects(ndx)
      [...]

      Set lblDay = getDateLabelByDate(clipped.firstDate)

      margin = lblDay.Width \ 20
      l = lblDay.Left + margin
      w = lblDay.Width * clipped.duration - (2 * margin)
      t = Locals.timelineForm.Controls(ROW_LABEL & .myLane).Top
      h = Locals.timelineForm.Controls(ROW_LABEL &
      .myLane).Height
      With .myLabel
        If (.Top <> t) Then .Top = t
        If (.Left <> l) Then .Left = l
        If (.Width <> w) Then .Width = w
        If (.Height <> h) Then .Height = h
        If Not .Visible Then .Visible = True
      End With

      Set lblDay = Nothing
```

```
    End If
  End With

End Sub
```

We use redundant Ifs to avoid useless assignments, to save some CPU cycles, but most of all to reduce the annoying flashes on the screen when the properties are set.

4. Else (object must not be shown)

Now, what happens if the object falls outside the visible timeline?

5. If it has a label, reclaim it

If it has an assigned label (because it was visible on the timeline), then it doesn't need it anymore. That's a waste of resources, so we can reclaim it and make it available for another object. First, we set it back to invisible and then release the associated pointer:

CLSTIMELINE

```
Private Sub drawObject(ndx As Integer)
  [...]

  With Objects(ndx)
      [...]

      Set lblDay = Nothing
    Else
      If Not (.myLabel Is Nothing) Then
        .myLabel.Visible = False
        Set .myLabel = Nothing
      End If
```

```
    End If
  End With
```

```
End Sub
```

And here it is. This function is over. But there's another obvious place where this function must be called, and that's when the whole timeline is redrawn, at the end of Redraw(), so that when the timeline is refreshed, all objects are reprocessed as well:

```
                        CLSTIMELINE
```

```
Private Sub Redraw()
[...]

  With Locals
    [...]
  End With

  For m = 1 To UBound(Objects)
    drawObject m
  Next

  DoEvents

End Sub
```

Since we are in Redraw(), there's one more improvement we can make. This function sets the visibility of several controls on the screen, and it's generally a good idea to disable the screen refresh until everything is done. This way, we can partly eliminate the typical tedious flickering, and we can also increase the overall speed a little bit:

CLSTIMELINE

```
Private Sub Redraw()
[...]
  Locals.timelineForm.Painting = False

  With Locals
    [...]
  End With

  For m = 1 To UBound(Objects)
    drawObject m
  Next

  DoEvents
  Locals.timelineForm.Painting = True

End Sub
```

This is actually a bit tricky. If the timeline is small and there are few objects, a normal modern computer should be able to handle the whole process extremely quickly. In this case, manipulating the .Painting property may even reduce the performance. It's generally a positive thing if the computer is slow, or the timeline has many lanes, or there are many objects on the screen at the same time. You may want to experiment with your specific case and decide whether it's better to keep it or remove it.

We're almost there! We just need one more function, assignLabel(), which finds and returns an available label. Luckily, this one is very simple. If you remember, we set all labels to invisible. So now, we just have to browse through all the controls on the calling form and find an invisible object label:

```
                          CLSTIMELINE

Private Function assignLabel() As Label
Dim retVal As Label
Dim ctl As Control

  Set retVal = Nothing

  For Each ctl In Locals.timelineForm.Controls
    If (ctl.Tag = "OBJECT") And Not ctl.Visible Then
      Set retVal = ctl
      Exit For
    End If
  Next

  Set assignLabel = retVal
  Set retVal = Nothing
  Set ctl = Nothing

End Function
```

And it's done. The class is now complete. I'm quite sure I lost you along the way; I know this is not easy to follow. It's not easy *per se*, it's a rather complicated algorithm, and it's not simple to organize it in a coherent and totally comprehensive way. But *verba manent*, as my ancestors used to say: *written words remain*, so you can read again the parts that are now unclear, and I'm sure that sooner or later, you'll be able to understand every single... bit. Another intended pun.

But let's make an example to see how this whole thing works.

Suppose we have a timeline with two months and two lanes only (Figure 5-22), to keep things simple.

	January	February
	Month 1	**Month 2**
Lane 1	= Lanes(1,1)	= Lanes(1,2)
Lane 2	= Lanes(2,1)	= Lanes(2,2)

Figure 5-22. *Placing an object: the timeline*

Let the first month be January and the second month February, just as an example.

The four slots of this array are Lanes(1,1) (the presence vector for Lane 1, Month 1), Lanes(1,2) (the vector for Lane 1, Month 2), Lanes(2,1) (the presence vector for Lane 2, Month 1), and Lanes(2,2) (the presence vector for Lane 2, Month 2). Their values are currently 0 because no object has been allocated yet, so the timeline is empty.

Now, let's explode the 0s in their binary representations (Figure 5-23), so we'll be able to see how the vectors work.

	January	February
	Month 1	**Month 2**
Lane 1	00000000000000000000000000000000	000000000000000000000000000000000
Lane 2	00000000000000000000000000000000	000000000000000000000000000000000

Figure 5-23. *Placing an object: the bit vectors*

Since we are using a long integer for each vector, we have 32 bits available, and see how this is perfect to "vectorize" our month days. There are 31 days for January, so the last bit will be unused. February has 28 days (or 29), so the last 4 (or 3) bits will be unused. As we said, each bit will be 1 if the corresponding day is occupied by an object, 0 otherwise.

Now, suppose we need to place an object whose life spans from January 29th to February 5th. Figure 5-24 shows the current value of Lanes(1,1) (which is 0) and the object mask for the first month (January), the value of which is stored in the variable we called objectMask(1), calculated in the function addObject() using buildMask(). The last three bits are set because the object lifespan intersects January on days 29, 30, and 31.

January																Bit (= day - 1)																
	n/a	30	29	28	27	26	25	24	23	22	21	20	19	18	17	16	15	14	13	12	11	10	9	8	7	6	5	4	3	2	1	0
Lanes(1,1)	0	0	0	0	0	0	0	0	0	0	0	0	0	0	0	0	0	0	0	0	0	0	0	0	0	0	0	0	0	0	0	0
objectMask(1)	0	1	1	1	0	0	0	0	0	0	0	0	0	0	0	0	0	0	0	0	0	0	0	0	0	0	0	0	0	0	0	0

Figure 5-24. *Placing an object: Lanes(1, 1)*

Now, we need to know if the January portion of Lane 1 is a suitable place for this object, that's to say if the three days we need are free or already occupied by another object. How can we do that? As we said, when we talked about the bit-field technique, we can AND the lane vector with the object mask (Figure 5-25).

January																Bit (= day - 1)																
	n/a	30	29	28	27	26	25	24	23	22	21	20	19	18	17	16	15	14	13	12	11	10	9	8	7	6	5	4	3	2	1	0
Lanes(1,1)	0	0	0	0	0	0	0	0	0	0	0	0	0	0	0	0	0	0	0	0	0	0	0	0	0	0	0	0	0	0	0	0
objectMask(1)	0	1	1	1	0	0	0	0	0	0	0	0	0	0	0	0	0	0	0	0	0	0	0	0	0	0	0	0	0	0	0	0
AND	0	0	0	0	0	0	0	0	0	0	0	0	0	0	0	0	0	0	0	0	0	0	0	0	0	0	0	0	0	0	0	0

Figure 5-25. *Placing an object: first month*

In this case, Lane(1,1) AND objectMask(1) = 0. This 0 tells us that there is room to accommodate our object on the January portion of Lane 1 (which is in fact empty).

Let's do the same for February, which is represented by the second column in our Lanes() array, to check if there's space to allocate the February portion of the object (Figure 5-26).

February   Bit (= day - 1)

				27	26	25	24	23	22	21	20	19	18	17	16	15	14	13	12	11	10	9	8	7	6	5	4	3	2	1	0
Lanes(1,2)	0	0	0	0	0	0	0	0	0	0	0	0	0	0	0	0	0	0	0	0	0	0	0	0	0	0	0	0	0	0	0	0
objectMask(2)	0	0	0	0	0	0	0	0	0	0	0	0	0	0	0	0	0	0	0	0	0	0	0	0	0	0	0	1	1	1	1	1

Figure 5-26. *Placing an object: second month*

Here, we only have 28 days – supposing we're not dealing with a leap year – so the last 4 bits are unused. In February, the object occupies days 1, 2, 3, 4, and 5, and the value for this mask is stored in objectMask(2).

Since this is the first object we place, the lanes are empty, and the AND with the lane's vector gives 0 again: this means that the five days we need in February are available.

What we found is that Lane 1 can host the whole object, so we can place it on it, assigning it a label, setting its size and position, and making it visible, as we saw earlier in the code.

Now, we have to update the lane's vector to mark all these days as "occupied" (Figure 5-27) so that they won't be made available for any other object. How can we do that? Raising the corresponding bits, using an OR. Let's do it for January.

January   Bit (= day - 1)

		30	29	28	27	26	25	24	23	22	21	20	19	18	17	16	15	14	13	12	11	10	9	8	7	6	5	4	3	2	1	0
Lanes(1,1)	0	0	0	0	0	0	0	0	0	0	0	0	0	0	0	0	0	0	0	0	0	0	0	0	0	0	0	0	0	0	0	0
objectMask(1)	0	1	1	1	0	0	0	0	0	0	0	0	0	0	0	0	0	0	0	0	0	0	0	0	0	0	0	0	0	0	0	0
OR	0	1	1	1	0	0	0	0	0	0	0	0	0	0	0	0	0	0	0	0	0	0	0	0	0	0	0	0	0	0	0	0

Figure 5-27. *Placing an object: updating the vectors (first month)*

And put this value into Lanes(1,1):

Lanes(1,1) = 01110000000000000000000000000000

Now, if you're curious to know what the actual value for this variable is, just type ? Lanes(1,1) in the Immediate Window, and you'll get an overwhelming 30.064.771.072. The good thing is that we don't care at all about the actual (decimal) values of our vectors, as we never have to deal with them. It suffices to know that they are valid values for our Long variables, and that's it.

We do the same with February: first, an OR to raise the bits of the occupied days (Figure 5-28).

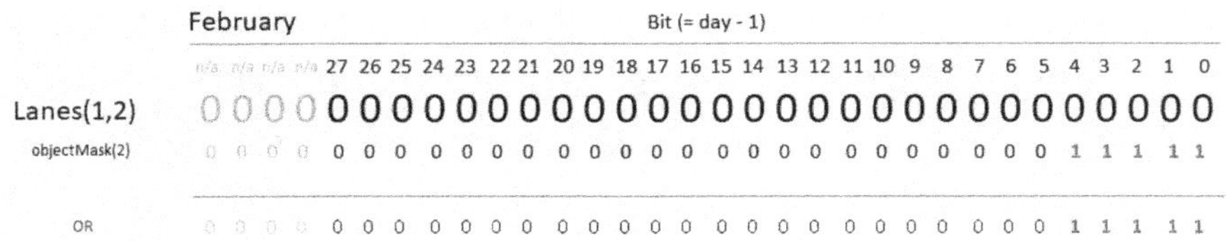

Figure 5-28. *Placing an object: updating the vectors (second month)*

and assign this value to Lane(1,2):

Lanes(1,2) = 00000000000000000000000000011111

For the curious, the decimal equivalent is a more comfortable 31. But again, we don't really care. The process for this object is done.

Now, let's say a second object arrives, whose life spans from February 3rd to February 15th.

Again, we have to place it somewhere. January is not involved in this process, as its intersection with the object lifespan is clearly void, so allow me to skip the checks on January, and just focus on February. We start from Lane 1 to check whether it has room enough to accommodate our new object. This means making an AND between the current lane vector and the object mask (Figure 5-29).

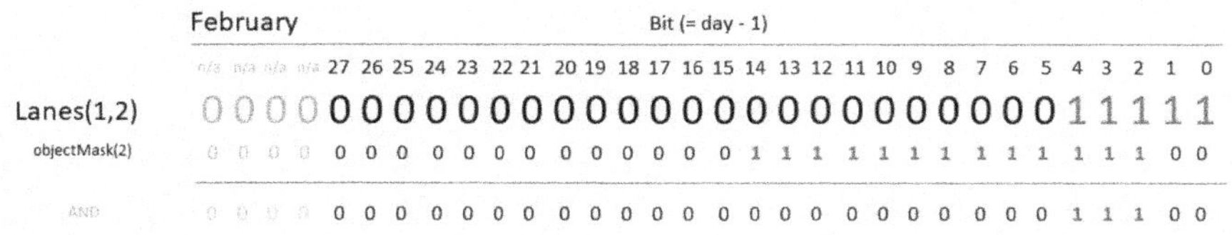

Figure 5-29. *Placing a second object: overlap*

And this time, we see that the AND is not 0. This means that some or all of the days our object needs in this month are already occupied – in this case, days 3, 4, and 5 are not available, as those are the days already assigned to the first object. So, Lane 1 is not available to host our second object.

Then we have to start the whole process again on the second lane, performing the same operations. Since Lane 2 is currently empty, our search will finish, selecting Lane 2 for this second object. If, on the contrary, we had a nonzero result, we'd know that the second lane is occupied as well, and we could proceed to the third, and then the fourth, and then the others, until we find one or just run out of lanes.

We are ready to go. We just have to add some objects, so go to the Form_Load() event and type:

```
                                FORM

Option Explicit

Private Sub Form_Load()
  Set TML = New clsTimeline
  TML.Init Me

  TML.addObject "Object 1", #7/25/2024#, 10
  TML.addObject "Object 2", #8/12/2024#, 5

End Sub
```

Since the timeline starts by centering "today," you'd better replace the two dates with dates closer to your "today" at the moment you're reading.

You should see the two objects properly placed (Figure 5-30) and "anchored" to the timeline, so they scroll along with it. That's because each time a scroll button is pressed, the function Redraw() is called, which redraws the timeline and then recalls drawObjects() to reprocess all the objects, resizing, repositioning, distributing and recalling labels, and setting all labels' visibility.

Figure 5-30. *Objects on the timeline*

You may notice an annoying flickering of buttons and labels, but this is how Access handles the screen, and there's not much we can do about it, more than what we already did, using those redundant Ifs and setting the .Painting property of the form to False (by the way, try eliminating this last one; in this particular case, the performance should increase…).

And now let's force an overlap. Add one more object:

```
                                    FORM

Option Explicit

Private Sub Form_Load()
  Set TML = New clsTimeline
  TML.Init Me

  TML.addObject "Object 1", #7/25/2024#, 10
  TML.addObject "Object 2", #8/12/2024#, 5
  TML.addObject "Object 3", #8/2/2024#, 8
End Sub
```

And run the form again.

Now, this third object overlaps with Object 1 over two days (Figure 5-31), so it couldn't be placed on the first lane. And in fact, it has been correctly placed on the second lane.

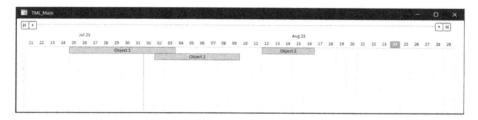

Figure 5-31. *Overlapping objects*

5.5. Conclusion

Well, it's been quite a long ride, but the result is something... "different" from the usual interfaces made with text boxes, combo boxes, labels, and so on. Though not perfect, and not always applicable, and with some limitations, I think this is a great way to show temporal information.

Of course, again, I had to simplify a lot. For example, some checks are missing but also a number of possible functionalities such as

- Scrolling by month or quarter

- The possibility to dynamically extend the timeline

- The possibility to hide and show single objects or "mark" them with different graphical styles

- Making the objects draggable

and more can be implemented, but I decided to keep them out of here to simplify this example to the bone.

CHAPTER 6

Outro

So, this is the end. A long ride indeed, not always comfortable, and many topics we discussed probably were not so simple as one could wish for. But hey, we're talking about *advanced* VBA!

Anyway, worst-case scenario, this is what you can take home from this book:

- A class to make images draggable

- A class to implement a "sliding doors" effect

- A class to manipulate binary vectors to implement the bit-field technique

- A class to add a scrollable timeline (with objects) to your projects

So, even if you don't understand every single line (yet!), you still have something to spice up your Access applications. And I'm pretty sure that going through all the pages again and again, finally you'll find how to master the whole thing. I'm not more intelligent than you, I just spent more time than you on this stuff.

At this point, your imagination is your limit. Combining the timeline with the dragging technique will open new horizons and new possibilities. The bit-field technique, sooner or later, will reveal its great potential in a huge number of different situations.

So, I do hope this book hasn't failed your expectations. Please don t hesitate to contact me and let me know if you found it useful, or totally useless, or anything in between. But never stop trying, never stop experimenting, never stop looking for new ideas. Access is already a rather despised software; let's all try to create something more interesting than just a usual bunch of flat forms with text boxes, command buttons, and endless tables of records. I know, Access is not a graphical system, and maybe the things we saw in this book represent its limits, and maybe nothing more can be done.

Or can it? It's up to us.

Index

A

Abstraction, 43
Access file, 29, 227
Access project, 187
Add(), 140
As New version, 32, 33
assignLabel() function, 253

B

Binary-based technique, 13
Binary masks, 70
Binary number, 67
"Bit-field" technique, 13, 227, 241
Blocks, 25, 26
Boolean, 34, 35, 89
Boolean parameters, 12–16
ByVal, 40

C

Caller variable, 135
Call instruction, 39, 40
Camel Case, 5
CDate(), 35
Class_Initialize() event, 58
Class instantiation, 47

Class properties
  GET, 52
  LET, 51
  SET, 53, 54
clientName, 6
clsInvitees, 58
clsMaster object, 128, 141, 147
clsMeeting, 58
clsSlave, 136–138
COBOL, 10
colorToday() function, 208
Comment, 23–28
"Companion" code module, 59
Connect multiple images
  Add(), 131, 140
  Caller variable, 135
  change MAX_IMAGES to
    5/create links, 148
  clsMaster object, 128, 131,
    141, 147
  clsSlave, 128, 133, 137, 138
  createLink(), 132, 141
  design, 128
  Edge() array, 141
  examples, 149
  Form_Load() event, 130
  getFreeLine(), 144

© The Editor(s) (if applicable) and The Author(s),
under exclusive license to APress Media, LLC, part of Springer Nature 2024
A. Grimaldi, *Advanced interactive interfaces with Access*,
https://doi.org/10.1007/979-8-8688-0808-1

Connect multiple images (*cont.*)
Init() function, 134, 136
lin, 146
master-slave technique, 133
MAX_IMAGES, 129
Moved() function, 136, 145
physical control, form, 138
placeLink() function, 146
recEdge.ctl, 138
recEdge.targetImageNdx, 138
slave object, 133, 141
Slaves(), 139
src and tgt, 142
src to tgt, 143
top-down approach, 130
WithEvents, 128, 131
worst-case scenario, 129
Connect two images with lines
Center() in clsDrag, 112
Center(), 110, 111
classes, 109
Connect(), 110, 112, 123, 124
connecting images, 108
events, 126
Form_Load(), 122
image centers, 110
line control, 109
MAX_IMAGES, 109
mouseMove(), 123, 126
placing a line, 113
private structures, 112
WithEvents, 124, 126
Control names, 17, 18
Control tags, 18, 19

Create() function, 168
createLink() function, 132

D

Date data type, 35
Denormalization, 56
Designing timeline
control names and tags, 189
day placeholders, 189
form, 188
lanes, 190
month labels, 189
text, 189
vertical lines, day seperators, 190, 191
vertical lines, month seperators, 191
Dim declaration, 49
Dim As New, 32–34
DoEvents, 163
Draggable image
add new image to form, 105–109
Boolean variable, 89
border, 97, 98
calculate new position, 96
class initialization, VBA, 91
create new database, 88
form creation, 88
Form Design.Insert.Image. Browse, 89
"init" function, 92
Load() event, 103
mouseDown() events, 93

mouseMove() event, 93, 95, 103, 104

mouseUp() events, 93, 95

myImage_mouseDown(), 93

new position, border, 98

objects with events, 90, 91

Single variables, 89

system restore point, 94

vertical axis, 101

WithEvents variable, 90

Dragging technique

connect multiple images, 127

connect two images with lines, 108

create "sliding forms" effect, 88

the "ghost label" technique, 150

master-slave structure, 164

sliding forms, 164

drawObjects(), 266

E

Edge() array, 141

Encapsulation, 43

Enumeration, 84

Exit point, function, 19–21

F

Feedback, 41

Form_Close(), 48

Form_Load() event, 122, 158

Function exit point, 19–21

Function returns value, 21–22

G

Garbage collection, 28

getFreeLine(), 144

GET property, 52

getRandomID(), 11

"ghost label" effect, 88

The "ghost label" technique

brand-new database, 153

design, 150

DoEvents, 163

drag, 152

filling levels, 163

Form_Load() event, 158

HyperlinkSubAddress property, 157

Init() function, 154

Intersect() function, 160, 161

mouseDown() event, 154

mouseMove(), 156, 159

mouseUp(), 157, 159

myLabel, 153

stacks, 152, 162

tgt is Nothing, 161

WithEvents, 160

GoTo, 20, 21

"Graphical" comments, 28

H

HyperlinkSubAddress property, 157

I, J

imgDrag2, 105
Indent, 23–28
Inheritance, 44
Init() function, 103, 134, 136, 154, 171, 230
initApp(), 47
Initialize() event, 59
In-line approach, 31
Intersect() function, 160, 161
isOK, 6
itemCodeNumber, 6

K

Kebab case, 5

L

LET property, 51
Load() event, 103
Logical bitwise operations, 67

M

Mask, 70
Master-slave technique, 171
mouseDown() event, 154
mouseMove() event, 95, 104
mouseUp(), 157
Moved() function, 136, 145
myFunc(parm1, parm2) function, 39
myImage_mouseDown() events, 93

N

Navigation controls
    Boolean variable, 218, 222
    class termination, 220
    cmdNext, 224
    cmdPrev_MouseDown(), 223
    constants, 217
    enableAll() function, 225
    gotoDate() function, 220, 223, 227
    MAX_DATE, 217
    mouseDown event, 220
    mouseUp() event, 223
    requirements, 217
    WithEvents objects, 218
Nested classes, 57–63
Number-of-registered-clients, 5

O

Object destruction, 28, 29
Object-oriented programming (OOP) language, 42, 43
    definition, 43
    examples, 44
    principles, 43
Objects placing in timeline
    addObject(), 232
    assigned label, 257
    assignLabel() function, 259
    binary arithmetic, 250
    bit vectors, 231, 232
    buildMask() function, 241, 248

clipInterval(), 233, 239, 245
clipped.assignLabel()
    function, 253
clipped.Duration, 252
Date data type, 228
DateSerial(), 238
drawObject(), 245, 251
enmVectorMasks, 231
first iteration, 249
Form_Load() event, 230
isOK object, 244
isOn() class method, 243
labels, 228
Lanes() array, 229
lblDay, 254
loop variable, 240
MIN_DATE, 236
objectMasks(), 241
object name, 232
object's lifespan, 234, 242
object width, 255
objMonthDays(), 236
overlapping, 264–267
.Painting property, 259, 266
position, 255
Redraw(), 258
retVal, 250
slots, lanes, 261–263
storing properties, 229
updating vectors, 263, 264
whole timeline, 231
objMonthDays(m).Duration, 245
OOP programming language, 43
OOP's isolation requirement, 56

Optional parameters, 16
Option Compare, 4
Option Compare Binary (default), 3
Option Compare Database, 3
Option Compare Text, 3

P, Q

ParamArray, 173
Pascal case, 5
placeLink() function, 146
Polymorphism, 44
Presence vector technique
    assigning bits, 69
    binary number, 67
    binary number
        conversion, 84–86
    bit-by-bit operation, 79
    Bit vector, 69
    decimal operation, 80
    definition, 65
    enumeration, 76
    example, 65
    Hex code, 78
    iterations, 76
    logical bitwise operations, 67
    mask, 70, 78
    single byte, 68
    table structure, 66
    three-table query, 66, 69
    empty vector V, 70
    vector class initialization, 80–84
Private/public, 7
Public structure, 50, 56

R

recEdge.ctl, 138
Redraw() function, 201, 212
retVal variable, 21

S

Screaming Snake Case, 5
Scrollable timeline
    code, 191
    colorToday(), 213
    "companion module"
        concept, 193
    crtDate() function, 208
    date selection, 199
    day intervals, 193
    day label, 192
    DoEvents, 212
    Form_Load() event, 194
    form module, 194
    fractions of months
        detection, 203
    getDateLabelByDate(), 215
    getDateLabelByPos() function,
        207, 212
    goToDate() function, 198
    Init() function, 194
    isVisible() function, 214, 215
    master-slave technique, 195
    MAX_DATE, 216
    MIN_DATE, 215
    month labels, 202
    monthLimits() function, 209
    month name labels, 193

    resize and caption labels, 210
    specified date, 199
    storing reference, 198
    timeline boundaries, 192
    TML the (public) instance, 194
    duration, 194
    variables, 196
    visible time window, 202
    visible window boundaries, 201
SELECT CASE, 36, 37, 39
Service function, 11, 12
Set instruction, 28
SET property, 53, 54
Slaves(), 139
Sliding forms, 164
    add doEvents, 184
    adjacent subforms, 164
    caller handle, 180
    Caller, 173
    calling handle, 180
    clsHandle_Slave, 167
    Create() function, 168, 171
    design, 166
    example, 165
    Form_Load() event, 167, 185
    handle movement, 176, 181, 182
    Init() function, 168, 171, 172
    isResizing variable, 175
    master class, 167, 169
    master-slave technique, 171
    mouseMove(), 176
    mouseUp(), 178
    Moved() method, clsHandle_
        Master, 178

n subforms, 166
ParamArray, 173
potential position, handle, 180
properties, 184
subforms, 164–166
WithEvents variable, 174
Space, 23–28

T

Temporal relations, 187
Terminate() event, 92
Test() function, 40
Top-down approach, 130, 141

U

User-defined type (UDT), 9,
    10, 15, 89
User experience, 41

V

Variable names, 4–7
Variant, 34, 40
VBA class
    companion
        module, 55–57
    creation, 46
    disadvantages, 44, 45
    instantiation, 47, 48
    methods, 54, 55
    OOP elements, 44
    OOP language, 44
    properties, 49–51

W, X, Y, Z

Wall of declarations, 29–32
WithEvents variable, 90, 160

GPSR Compliance
The European Union's (EU) General Product Safety Regulation (GPSR) is a set
of rules that requires consumer products to be safe and our obligations to
ensure this.

If you have any concerns about our products, you can contact us on

ProductSafety@springernature.com

In case Publisher is established outside the EU, the EU authorized
representative is:

Springer Nature Customer Service Center GmbH
Europaplatz 3
69115 Heidelberg, Germany